The Right Brain Way

DRIVE YOUR BRAND WITH
THE POWER OF EMOTION

Charles T. Kenny, Ph.D.

Order this book online at www.trafford.com
or email orders@trafford.com

Most Trafford titles are also available at major online book retailers.

Cover Design by John Lambert

Print information available on the last page.

ISBN: 978-1-4251-3041-1 (sc)
ISBN: 978-1-4251-3042-8 (hc)
ISBN: 978-1-4251-3043-5 (e)

Trafford rev. 08/11/2016

 www.trafford.com

North America & international
toll-free: 1 888 232 4444 (USA & Canada)
fax: 812 355 4082

Praise For *The Right Brain Way*

Victor E. Zast, *President, Private Perfumery*
"In the competition for the consumer's attention, restricting yourself to conventional marketing research is like entering into a fight with one-half of your brain tied behind your back."

Jim Belasco, Ph.D., *Business Leadership Strategist and Best-Selling Author*
"*The Right Brain Way* is the key to finding the magic inside the minds of your customers. It will forever change the way you sell your brand. Dr. Charles Kenny's Right Brain Research can show you what business you're really in and exactly why your customers know more about it than you do. *The Right Brain Way* is a strategic road map to buried treasure. Read it and discover yours...inside the minds of your customers."

Peter Herschend, *Co-Founder & Co-Owner, Herschend Family Entertainment*
"Without a good sense of what your customer believes, knows and dreams about your business, you don't stand much of a chance of walking through "the door" that will match who you are to those same beliefs, knowledge or dreams. Charles Kenny and **Right Brain** offer all of us a way to step through that door and into the minds of those wonderful people we call customers."

Don Schultz, *Professor Emeritus of Integrated Marketing Communication, Northwestern University*
"*The Right Brain Way* illustrates how to *REALLY* gather customer feelings and beliefs so you can understand and make the most of them. Many promise a 'how to' way to generate customer insights. *The Right Brain Way* delivers."

3

John Meyers, *Director, Business Analysis & Information, Amgen*
"Read this book and discover how to create a winning product platform by removing the bias associated with traditional market research."

Tom Marnell, *President, MDM, Marketing Consultant and Database Architect*
"If you are a CEO today, your ignorance is killing you. The ineffectiveness of traditional research to give you what you really need to set strategic direction should either be driving you crazy or scaring you to death. Knowing your current customers and your next customers intimately is the only path to a sustainable strategic advantage in today's hyper-competitive marketplace. Dr. Kenny and *The Right Brain Way* can put you on that path."

Jim Neidorf, *President, Neidorf Concepts, LLC*
In the race to capture customer loyalty and market share, Right Brain Research is "the key" to the ignition. Without it, you just get into your vehicle, grab the steering wheel, make loud noises and pretend you're winning, but you're not *really* going anywhere. My advice: Read this book and turn the *Right Brain Key* before your competition does.

Michael J. Nussbaum, *President, Warehouse Connection*
Salespeople would do themselves a great service to read this book and learn that there is so much more to sales than personality. *The Right Brain Way* can take an average salesperson and show him why he's average. If he would incorporate *The Right Brain Way* of selling, he could then focus on doing what he needs to do and be vastly more successful.

Ken Kring, *Senior Manager of Strategy, at a Major Retailer*
"Anyone who is in business or interested in business should read this book. Right Brain Research will help you get at market and consumer behavioral truths that you cannot get at in any other way.

We choose The Right Brain Approach because it is the only way we know of to get at the information we need. If you are a CEO, I strongly encourage you to read *The Right Brain Way* before you spend any additional resources on product development, research, marketing or advertising. If you don't do this you risk allocating company resources in a sub-optimal and wasteful way. Why put your resources at risk when it's not necessary?"

Heidi Wanaski, *Marketing Director, Humira, Abbott Laboratories*
"I will never work on a new product introduction without having Right Brain at my side. We had more than a million dollars in the budget for marketing research. Most of it was wasted. We should have allocated a lot more of the budget for Right Brain."

Thomas M. Wittenschlaeger, *Chairman and Chief Executive Officer, Raptor Networks Technology, Inc.*
"I am outspoken in crediting a great many competitive wins and accompanying career successes to the depth of knowledge and radically different frame of reference we were able to acquire through Right Brain Research. People wonder, to this day, HOW my team won virtually every new business competition we pursued. Our team's competitive tenacity, depth of competitive analysis and preparation, and the 'secret weapon' of Right Brain Research's insights into the emotion-centric manner in which even the most senior executives make acquisition decisions proved to be a potent and winning combination. On every occasion where I called upon Dr. Kenny and the Right Brain People, we "T-Boned" the competition! They never saw it coming…Ironically, they ascribed their losses—my wins—to 'luck!'"

Dedication

In recognition and love for two of the best grandparents ever:

Mary Kalt Kenny & Frank Matonis

Whose love and devotion made it possible for their
descendants to become who they are.

>—•>—0—<•—<

And in recognition and love for the best
parents a man could ask for:

Anna C. Matonis Kenny & Charles T. Kenny, Sr.

Who inspired me in ways that I cannot even articulate!

Acknowledgements

I have been blessed with a wonderful group of friends whom I have come to call my "Literary Circle." These people gave their time generously to read the initial drafts and gave me detailed feedback. This experience was one of the very best parts of writing this book, because I was touched by the care and interest shown by each and every one of the people in the Circle. They include:

Tony Aretz	Tim Key	Doug Milliken	Bengt Sjogren
Larry Barnes	Ken Kring	Dan Moy	Ken Stevens
Jim Belasco	Carl Landwehr	Mike Nussbaum	Skip Thurnauer
Kurt Engelbrecht	Neil Lichtman	Jim Neidorf	Tom Wittenschlaeger
Renee Frigo	Tom Marnell	Bevalee Pray	
Pete Herschend	Mary Mazza	Thomas Rudkins	Victor E. Zast
Doug Kelly	John Meyers	Don Schultz	

Of course the responsibility for the final content is mine, but the book is immeasurably better because of the contributions of the Literary Circle. I have also been blessed with a wonderful team of editors, all of whom have made substantive contributions to the book:

Michelle Gagne Ballard	Randy Jelinek
Julie Leicester	Erin Walter
Heather Wilson	

I would like to acknowledge and thank the following people who have made substantive contributions to the success of Right Brain projects over the past 36 years:

Pete Ceren	Ronica Brown	Erin Walter
Kevin Duke	Diane Loeffler	Joy Ward
Lewis Evans	Mary Samuelson	Heather Wilson
Laura Faught		

I want to thank my support staff, the people whose work allows me to do two or three things at a time. Thanks to all for their dedication, their help and their advice. This book would never have been born without their contributions:

Christy Bosi | Karen Clough | Ellen Wherry

And thanks to Randy Jelinek for all of his great work directing the production and marketing of the book. Finally, I wish to send a note of special thanks to Tom Wittenschlaeger for his wonderful Foreword.

To all who read this book, I hope that you find the key to your own success in *The Right Brain Way*.

Charlie

Charles T. Kenny, Ph.D.
April, 2008

8

Table of Contents

Foreword: An Epiphany

Thomas M. Wittenschlaeger, Chairman and CEO,
Raptor Networks Technology, Inc.

Of all the positions that I've been privileged to serve in over the years, the most intellectually challenging, and the most fun, came from my time at the Hughes Aircraft Company — the technological gem founded by Howard Hughes to support his passion for racing aircraft. Howard Hughes founded the Hughes Aircraft Company in the early 1930s. He assembled the finest engineers in the world, because he wanted to build the fastest airplanes in the world. Standards that we take for granted today in aviation, such as flush rivets, fully enclosed cockpits and retractable landing gear, were all invented at the Hughes Aircraft Company to accomplish Howard's goals. It comes as no surprise, then, that Howard Hughes held the transcontinental speed record for more than 12 years.

Hughes was structured as a non-profit company, owned by the Howard Hughes Medical Foundation. After providing the medical foundation several hundred million dollars a year to advance the state of the art in medicine, Hughes Aircraft Company invested its residual earnings in technology and people. They had the best of both.

When entering corporate headquarters for the first time, visitors walked into a cavernous foyer in which massive satellites were suspended from the three story high ceiling, evoking a visceral response, indicating that their time at Hughes would be different from any other. The place was dripping with technology. Everywhere you looked, you could see the latest lasers, torpedoes, missiles, spacecraft and sensors. And the people — they were different too. Hughes had compiled more raw brain power than any of its competitors. They were brilliant, they were iconoclastic and they could think outside the box. Like Howard, they were rebels.

When I was promoted to Director of the corporate market research function at Hughes, I came across Right Brain Research. Unlike most market research professionals, I had come from the line organizations, where I had started in systems engineering and later ran the business development teams of some of Hughes' most successful divisions. Also, unlike most marketing, advertising and sales professionals, I was an electrical and nuclear engineer and former submarine officer, who was dragged kicking and screaming into a marketing role—a role I viewed as perfectly incongruent with my personal strengths. My mentor at that time was Toby Warson, who later became President of Honeywell. He used to quip, "Marketing is easy to do—it's just hard to do well." At Hughes Aircraft, I was assigned to the market research role to help "less winning" divisions figure out how to capture more new business. I had little time or patience for effusive branding "experts" and squishy advertising agencies.

When I met Charlie, I knew he was different—very, very different. There were no flashy, shiny brochures or cutesy videos to sell his approach. Dr. Kenny exuded the understated scholarly confidence and rumpled demeanor of a deep thinker. He and I got along immediately. It helped that my alma mater, the United States Naval Academy, and his alma mater, Notre Dame, were "sister" schools. But, it helped even more that I felt he was introducing me to something very special, almost **revolutionary**.

The first challenge we worked on together took us to the absolute edge of technological innovation: The Strategic Defense Initiative (SDI) or "Star Wars" Project, as it had been called under President Ronald Reagan. Hughes was a "natural" to win research and development projects in this vital national initiative, because of its technology leadership in optical and non-optical sensors as well as in weapons control and large-scale systems architectures. What we observed in practice, alarmingly, was quite different. Hughes was winning far less business than it should have, considering its inventive prowess. We needed a rigorous diagnostic assessment of why we were falling short in the eyes of the customer, and we needed it quickly.

I had been looking for a different way to understand the inconsistency between Hughes' clear "raw science" advantage and the lack of success in winning contracts in this new field. I was prepared to do whatever it took to figure it out. I flew to Memphis for a demonstration of the Right Brain Research methodology. I observed three live interviews, postulated what insights the approach might generate and assessed whether the methodology could be reasonably deployed into an area as secretive and impenetrable as the Strategic Defense Initiative. While we laugh about it now, it annoyed Dr. Kenny to no end that I seemed to be paying less attention to the interviewing process than he believed would be required to "win me over." He was wrong. Unbeknownst to him, I was having a quiet epiphany.

One week later, I invited Dr. Kenny back to Hughes corporate headquarters to discuss how The Right Brain Approach would be deployed to diagnose what was happening in the hearts and minds of our customers. We discussed recruiting the sample, training the interview team, hypotheses and how we would communicate the findings.

I was impatient. This was a very important project to Hughes, to my boss, and more importantly, to his boss, C. Michael Armstrong, the famed Hughes Chairman and CEO, who later would become CEO of AT&T. I was determined to crack the puzzle, build a "fix strategy" and brief it to operations without getting fired. You see, these truly brilliant technologists were very proud, did not take well to criticism, no matter how well intentioned, and had perfected the art of "shooting the messenger" when the messenger disagreed with their infallibility. Concluding two hours of intense discussions with Charlie, I opened my desk drawer, pulled out my corporate "priority projects" checkbook and wrote him a check on the spot, insisting his team start work on SDI immediately. You should have seen his face! He tells me that no client before or since has ever done that. It created a memorable moment in what would become a lifelong relationship of mutual respect.

Charlie's team faced several crucial challenges. The SDI decision makers in key project roles were completely inaccessible because their work was highly classified, thus introducing a unique wrinkle that would serve as a barrier to any successful assessment. Further, we (the research team) had no clearances or "need to know." So, we could NOT interview THEM! Snatching pragmatism from the jaws of impossibility, we hatched the idea of interviewing recently retired military officers who had served on SDI as a proxy for those in command at the time. The project launched with anxious anticipation.

The case cracked faster than a missile's skin on final impact. We discovered that Hughes had every necessary ingredient for success, but was crafting its message and approach precisely backwards. We discovered that joining the "family" of Star Wars contractors required acting like members of the family—not like the smart, spoiled nephew. When we changed our approach, we changed the result. Hughes won project after project, and I won the privilege to move into a Corporate Director's office, becoming the youngest director in the company.

The SDI project was the first foray into "exotic technologies" for The Right Brain People. It would not be their last.

Our next project using The Right Brain Approach was in the Air Traffic Control Business. Hughes was competing for a technical support contract with the FAA. We possessed every technical and programmatic qualification to excel with the FAA, but had been unsuccessful in establishing even a beachhead relationship.

Just as in the SDI project, we relied on proxies in lieu of senior FAA officials, although we were also able to interview some middle managers within the FAA itself. We discovered the dominant perception of Hughes within the FAA community—senior officials, middle managers and former FAA executives all felt strongly that the Hughes team simply did not respect them. Unbeknownst to top management at Hughes, our project teams were seen as hopelessly arrogant by the FAA. Therefore, our substantial investment in messaging that Hughes offered "SUPERIOR TECHNOLOGY," while true, was completely INEFFECTUAL.

The Right Brain People convinced a small group of us that we needed to shift the tone of our proposal, briefings and site visits to one of subservience, respect and support. This recommendation was extraordinarily difficult for the Hughes team to swallow. Under bruising disagreement from Hughes' technologists, program management and capture team leaders, I tone-shifted the proposal to the direction indicated by the Right Brain findings. It was a "bet your career" gamble. Some four months later Hughes was awarded the $200M FAA support contract!

The next time Dr. Kenny visited me, I was a Vice President and Assistant Division Manager of the Air Traffic Control Division at Hughes. I was responsible for running the organization. The division was just a $500M operation at that time, but we had ambitious goals. We learned that the next opportunity for us would be working with the FAA. The agency was planning its largest upgrade ever, to the STARS Program, which guides aircraft safely at altitudes of 24,500 feet and above. The program's purpose was to update the country's enroute air traffic control system. Again, Hughes sought to compete, but had stiff competition from Lockheed Martin and Raytheon, both of whom, while less technology-savvy, enjoyed entrenched and personal long-term relationships with the FAA.

Here, we used The Right Brain Approach to understand which of our two competitors would make the most persuasive strategic alliance in the eyes of the FAA. We discovered that should Hughes and each of its two competitors independently compete for the prime contract, Lockheed Martin would win. No question. The only chance Hughes had in winning was to team with its arch-nemesis, and HATED east coast rival, Raytheon.

The "conventional wisdom" at Hughes asserted that no such thing could be accomplished. The Right Brain Research showed a different picture; we discovered that the FAA would actually welcome a team arrangement. I flew to Massachusetts for a meeting with my counterpart at Raytheon. Just as my "experts" had told me that Hughes would win, his "experts" had told him Raytheon would win. BOTH sets of "experts" stated with unflinching confidence that Hughes and Raytheon could never reach agreement on teaming. Both sets of "experts" were dead wrong.

Knowing that it was important, and a point of corporate pride to Raytheon to be the prime contractor on this team, I was prepared to concede the prime role in return for Raytheon letting Hughes do what it did best. In sharp contrast to what every expert on both sides had forecast, we concluded a teaming agreement within five days. Raytheon primed the proposal with 51% of the program content (and responsibility for the highest-risk, lowest margin integration elements of the project) with Hughes in a 49% support role, responsible for the lowest risk and most profitable elements.

Needless to say, when the Raytheon-Hughes team crushed Lockheed Martin for a $1.6B win (yes…I said BILLION), people took notice. Lots of them. The STARS win proved to be a turning point in my career, and is still used to this day within Raytheon (which bought the Hughes ATC business) as a case study on winning major programs. I became a Corporate Vice President and known as a "turnaround guy." Today I serve as Chairman and CEO of a publicly traded, commercial, high technology company, and people still wonder HOW I won every major competition I touched.

I am outspoken in crediting my competitive wins and accompanying career success to the depth of knowledge and radically different frame of reference derived from Right Brain Research. I consider Dr. Kenny a mentor to my success. In my opinion, the spectacular successes that I spearheaded at Hughes were enabled by the discoveries provided by Right Brain Research and the uncompromising strategic action that we took based on the findings. Competitive tenacity coupled with customer insight unknown to the competition is a potent combination. At times, taking "outside the box" steps was very risky, but they always paid huge dividends. If that is the sort of impact you want to have, ***then the way to make it happen is to follow The Right Brain Way.***

On a personal note, I affectionately refer to Dr. Kenny as Dr. Charles "T-Bone" Kenny. He had assumed for years it was because we enjoyed a T-Bone dinner together almost a decade earlier, which proved to be half right. It evolved into a permanent label, he recently discovered, because on every occasion where I called upon Dr. Kenny's counsel, we would "T-Bone" the competition! They never saw it coming…they simply woke up dead! I guess that's a bit of the submariner in me talking.…

PART I

WHY THE RIGHT BRAIN WAY?

CHAPTER ONE

> ⊱┈•✦•┈⊰

"Why" Questions

"If you build it, they will come."
— FIELD OF DREAMS

In 1980 Bill Bernbach, the twentieth century advertising guru and founder of Doyle, Dane, Bernbach, currently in business as DDB Worldwide, spoke to the American Association of Advertising Agencies and startled his audience by calling for a new direction in advertising. In his speech, he encouraged his audience to emphasize emotion and move away from the rational approach to advertising so prevalent at the time.

Without fully realizing it, Bill Bernbach was issuing a call for emotional research.

Fast-forward to 2005, Don Schultz, one of the leading experts in branding, is conducting seminars at The Kellogg School of Management at Northwestern. He begins to tell his audiences of marketing and marketing research professionals that market research is dead. He says that people do not think, perceive, feel or behave in ways that fit the standard linear research models that currently dominate marketing research. He points out that the assumptions underlying the design of most market research methods are not consistent with the way people make decisions in the consumer marketplace.

Like Bill Bernbach before him, Don Shultz was issuing a call for research methods that are in line with how the consumer's mind works.

Despite Bernbach's challenge, why is it that 25 years later, so many businesses are still unable to uncover the true emotional motivators that drive consumer behavior? Inspired by Bernbach's message, advertising professionals sought new approaches to consumer research. They found a number of them such as grid techniques, projective techniques, laddering, ethnography, observational research, linguistic analysis, cultural "psychoanalysis," archetypes, brainwaves, pupilometry, dyads and triads. But in the end, these approaches do not elicit powerful new insights based on consumer emotion. They do not uncover the emotionally based information and depth of understanding that marketers need in order to build powerful brands.

Why do these other approaches not bring depth of understanding and powerful insights? The reason is that they do not answer questions about why people do what they do. They do not explain why people buy what they buy. Without this understanding of consumer motivation, marketers play guessing games as they formulate their strategies. However, there is a way to get the answers to "why" questions. This book describes and details The Right Brain Way for capturing consumer motivation and translating that understanding into valuable insights. We believe that the reader will find that market research is very much alive after all and that it is essential to the growth and development of any corporate enterprise or organization.

I first learned the importance of asking and answering "why" questions in business when I met Pete Herschend, co-owner and then Vice President of Marketing for Silver Dollar City, a theme park inspired by an Ozark mining town located in Branson, Missouri. (See chapter 14 for the story of the City.) I was an Industrial Psychologist serving on a 4-person team assembled by Pete to develop a 5-year strategic plan for the theme park. Pete asked me if I could tell him why people come to visit the City and why people come back year after year.

"Why do you want to know?" I asked. His objective was to figure out how to invest the company's retained earnings each year. His executive team generated hundreds of great ideas every year for improving and enlarging the theme park for the following season, but they could only implement a small portion of them. He wanted the answer to his "why" question to give the executive team a framework for prioritizing the long list of new ideas each year.

In short, he wanted help with decisions about how to invest in his brand. Of course he did. Every marketer, and every CEO for that matter, wants this important information. But, not all of them know how to get it. Fortunately, that is what this book is about.

I told Pete that in order to answer "why" questions it is necessary to uncover what motivates consumer behavior. And, since motivation is about emotion, I told him that he needed emotional research. At that time, however, there was no methodology for conducting emotional research!

No research or analysis existed except for academic theories of motivation that do not link directly to consumer decisions. Unfortunately, these theories did not include methods for answering questions about consumer motivation. So, we began to search for a methodology that would answer Pete's question. That search led down the path to developing Right Brain Research.

Pete's interest was not just in advertising and marketing. He was interested in the growth, direction and success of his business as a whole. Using our method, Pete found the answers to his question about why people come to the City. Over the years he has continued to ask "why" questions about different aspects of the business. Acting on the answers to these questions, he and his management team were able to breathe new life into all aspects of Silver Dollar City, watching it undergo an unprecedented spurt in growth (park attendance increased six-fold over the next 30 years). The answers helped everyone within the theme park develop stronger relationships with suppliers, prospects, customers and strategic partners, enriching and fortifying future financial transactions for everyone involved.

Understanding consumer motivation at the deepest level is an investment with broad-reaching benefits impacting all operational elements within an organization that tie into the brand in any way. The reality is that a company's brand is not only communicated through the marketing and sale of goods and services, it is communicated every single time the brand touches people, including employees, investors, suppliers, vendors, lenders and even passers-by. For this reason, answering "why" questions and using the consumer insight that comes with the answers is critical to directing a company's marketing, advertising and investment strategies as well as customer service, sales and supplier relationships. Emotional research is not an expense. It is an investment that brings financial returns many times over.

Answering "why" questions gives people within an organization insight into the consumer that provides strategic direction. As a strong secondary benefit, it builds consensus on the management team and instills confidence in the decisions people make. The results of Right Brain Research allow management and employees to make sound decisions and predict outcomes without resorting to trial and error. This strategic direction relieves stress and makes everyone's job a lot more fun!

This book is not solely about emotional research, nor is it just for researchers, or just for marketers, because it is not just about marketing. Instead, it is a book about how and why understanding the emotional side of the consumer is critical to business success in the 21st Century. Consider the movie *Field of Dreams*. Ray Kinsella, the main character in the movie, repeatedly hears a voice telling him, "If you build it, they will come." For him, the "it" is a baseball diamond in the middle of a valuable cornfield. But it is not just a ball field. It is a playing field upon which everyone's most important fantasies are realized. The overriding theme is the return of the banished hero, Shoeless Joe Jackson, to a redemptive state. The fantasy that the field represents is that everyone can have a second chance. The message is that people can make mistakes, fail and still have a second chance to do the right thing. In a word, redemption is possible. The field allows people to enter a world that is innocent and fair, which is rejuvenating and reassuring because it reconnects them to the purity of their youth. For business people, the "it" is any product or service that is designed around the emotional benefits people are seeking. When "it" is designed and built in this way, customers will come and they will come in droves.

This book shows how emotional research brings a competitive edge to business, by exploring why emotional research is critical, how the mind works and what Right Brain Research entails. With examples from projects that reach back to 1972 for companies in almost every industry as well as the non-profit sector, the stories and case histories in this book demonstrate that insight into the consumer's emotional makeup is crucial to long-term business success.

CHAPTER TWO

>⤟∘⤞⤞

What Is A Brand After All?

"The whole is greater than the sum of its parts."
— THE BASIC PRINCIPLE OF GESTALT
PSYCHOLOGY

The most famous gold rush in American history led directly to the building of the great city of San Francisco and immortalized the gold-mining Forty-Niners! Most Americans do not think of prospecting for gold these days, assuming that it is too late for them. However, there is a mother lode to be found that is much larger than the one found at Sutter's Creek in 1848. The golden opportunity in business is in differentiating products and services and then building them into brands.

In the modern era of product parity, cultivating the brand has the richest potential to help marketers gain an advantage over the competition. Marketers who recognize this potential can harvest great rewards. The challenge is that there are forces working against them. Most MBA courses miss out on the essence of what a brand really is at the deepest level in the minds and hearts of consumers. Therefore, we find that the essence of what a brand is all about is underemphasized in the marketing and research functions of most companies. The consequence is that most companies unnecessarily leave a great deal of money on the table as they go to market with their brands.

It took FedEx ten years to wake up and realize that their customers were telling them something significant when they said "Just FedEx it!" During this ten-year period of time, FedEx executives actively resisted changing the brand's name. Eventually, they realized that the transformation of Federal Express into a verb by the everyday language of their customers gave them an opportunity, so in 1994 they officially adopted FedEx as the name of the brand that is recognized as the worldwide standard for fast, reliable service. In 2000 Federal Express Corporation capitulated fully to the consumer mindset and changed the corporate name to FedEx Corporation.

FedEx has the unique competitive advantage of being a noun and a verb in the language that people use to talk about delivery companies. Its chief competitor does not. No one ever says "UPS it to me!" Simply put, FedEx owns the territory of "urgency" in the mind; UPS does not. So even if UPS had clever phraseology like FedEx, people would not transform the name into a verb or use it in any other creative way. FedEx owns the position. FedEx took the position first, and has held onto it by being faithful to its brand. Other examples of products that have become part of our everyday language are Xerox, Kleenex, Jell-O, Scotch Tape and Coke. In the UK, instead of saying "Vacuum the house," people transform their most popular vacuum cleaner brand into a verb and say "Hoover the house"—making it a perfect example of a brand owning specific territory in the consumer's mind.

One reason that FedEx owns the position of being the company that can be relied on with certainty is that FedEx invented overnight delivery. UPS did not. FedEx established itself as the leader in a new sub-category within the shipping industry, and even though the Post Office and UPS had been in the business of shipping packages for generations before FedEx came along, they had to play catch up and offer the same services that FedEx offered.

So, how did FedEx establish its brand as the leader? FedEx started its first national advertising campaign by showing people that the company had trucks and planes. In 1973 and 1974 corporate shipping departments around the USA tested FedEx by shipping large quantities of empty boxes around the country, because they found the promise of overnight delivery so tantalizing, yet preposterous. FedEx was in stage one of a company's development; they were simply trying to prove that they were for real! Here, they were able to prove they could deliver a package to nearly anywhere in America overnight. Up to this point in time, they were engaged in a left brain campaign.

Then they moved to stage two. They entered into a right brain advertising campaign by demonstrating the emotional benefit of their unique service. FedEx began to recognize on some level that their service fulfilled customers' emotional needs. So, they designed the campaign to show consumers how their service fulfilled these needs. Their campaign employed humor and absurdities to show decision makers in American business that they could be risking their jobs if they did not send their packages overnight by FedEx. In a particularly hilarious thirty second commercial, the decision maker who chose an inferior shipping company is shown cowering and sniveling underneath the vanity skirt of a desk as the boss is running up and down the hall while ranting and raving about a package that a customer had expected but had still not received.

The campaign conveyed the message that FedEx is the one and only shipper that can provide people with reassurance and peace of mind that their packages will arrive the next morning. The FedEx brand is synonymous with reliability. FedEx means that your package will arrive the next day—"Absolutely, Positively" without a doubt. The reason humor was so effective is that the message keyed into people's fears of failure and judgment. Instead of saying, "You will be fired if you do not hire our company to deliver your packages," the ads demonstrated the potentially humiliating and damaging consequences of choosing a shipper that is not focused on reliably delivering packages overnight as FedEx is.

So, what is a brand after all? A brand is built upon the connection between the attributes of the product and the experience the consumer has buying and using the product. It is based on the difference between the literal product and what people are actually buying in terms of emotional benefits. The FedEx brand is not just the planes and trucks and employees. No matter how efficient and productive the equipment and people are, these things are just the price of being in business. All of these things are concrete and literal. They are all left brain. These things are necessary for the FedEx brand to exist. But if you look at each piece individually, you will never understand what makes the FedEx brand resonate with people. These components are not enough for the brand to spring forth. The brand is greater than the sum of its parts. It is not tangible, but it is nonetheless real because it is meaningful emotionally to the consumer.

The essence of a brand is always understood by the answer to the question: "What business are you really in?" For example, FedEx is not merely in the business of providing overnight shipping services. The company is really in the business of providing customers with reassurance and peace of mind. The business that the company is really in is what its brand is all about. Most companies have an incomplete answer to the question of what business they are really in. And that is why there is so much confusion over what a brand really is. The way to discover the answer is to delve into the mind of the consumer and understand at an emotional level what motivates people to buy.

The word "brand" was used on the frontier when ranchers burned their mark into the sides of their cattle. The mark helped them to discourage rustling on the open range and helped them separate their cattle from the others at the railhead and at market. This history is the origin of the mark, brand or logo as it has come to be called. The origin of brand is literal and concrete, so why is it elusive and why is it poorly understood? Why are there so many different perceptions of what it has come to mean over time and how it operates in the marketplace? The reason is that the products and services that are sold are concrete; they can be seen. Brand is abstract. Brand is conceptual. A brand cannot be seen — not literally seen, although its manifestations can be seen, especially if one knows where and how to look.

Properly understood and acted upon by marketers, brand is the most valuable management tool available to them for enriching their businesses. It is the cornerstone on which to build value that can be seen in the marketplace, in the store, on websites and on Wall Street.

When stumbling into an elusive concept like brand, it is helpful, in fact necessary, to understand what it is not. With that understanding firmly in place, a meaningful definition can be formulated.

Here are some of the things that a brand is not:

• Brand is not a logo

• Brand is not a name

• Brand is not a theme line

• Brand is not the advertising

These things may be part of a brand, but they are certainly not equivalent to the brand. They simply do not capture the heart of what a brand means, yet all four are confused with brand and melded into it every day.

There are many dimensions and concepts that are related to brand that marketers talk about. These dimensions overlap with one another. Different marketers mean different things by them and so there is no unanimity and much confusion. Some marketers even mistakenly equate one or more of them to brand. Here are some of the dimensions that marketers talk about:

• Brand awareness
   Unaided
   Aided

- Brand image
- Brand attributes
- Brand equity
- Brand loyalty
- Brand identity
- Brand essence
- Brand character
- Brand position
- Brand value
- Brand touch points
- Brand steward
- Brand manager
- Brand management
- Brand extension

Two others come to mind—dimensions that have come into more common usage recently as more attention is being paid to brand. They are:

- Brand language
- Brand promise

The proliferation of language about brand indicates a lot of concern and interest in brand, but there are so many terms that the core of what a brand is all about gets lost all too often in the chatter—chatter which often becomes a cacophony of words and phrases without depth and understanding.

When brand is understood at its core, it becomes the primary engine for leveraging a business. Therefore, brand is not or should not be "owned" by marketing. The best brands, the ones with the most value in the marketplace, are directed by the CEO, not by the marketing department.

Jack Welch is half right about the job of the CEO. As he defines it, the job of the CEO is to hire and develop the best possible people. But, he missed the other half of the job! It is to make sure that the people he hires nourish the company brands for which they are responsible. Group VPs and Directors cannot "subcontract" the responsibility to their marketing departments or to their ad agencies. When they do so, they do it at their own peril and the peril of the stockholders.

In order for executives and managers to see the potential for each of their businesses, a good definition of brand is essential. Many definitions of brand exist that focus on the literal aspects of brand. Therefore, we formulated our own definition that captures the true essence, power and potential of a brand. Our definition is as follows:

A brand is created as people make an emotional connection that transforms the literal product or service into an implicit promise that drives their perceptions, the way they feel, their behavior and their expectations.

The Gestalt psychologists said that the whole is greater than the sum of the parts. They meant that what people perceive is a function of both the actual visual images that they see and the expectations they impose on those images. A brand, then, is greater than the sum total of all of the product's attributes. The brand is that magical personality or essence that consumers grant to a product or service because of how it makes them feel.

The above definition of brand has the following elements that are not found in other definitions:

- A brand is *created* by people.
- A brand involves an *emotional connection*.
- People *transform* the product into an *implicit promise*.
- The implicit promise *drives feelings, behavior and expectations*.

The words in italics above are words that are not often found in MBA programs, in business textbooks or even in the popular business books that abound today. The reason that they are not in common usage in business is that these words are mostly right brain words, referring to right brain processes that in general are poorly understood compared to the left brain processes with which most business people are more familiar. And it is no wonder that most people are more familiar with them, for that is what formal education in the USA and most of the developed world is almost entirely based on—left brain skills and processes.

We address each of these elements and explain them, but first we want to single out a two-letter word in the definition—the word "as." The word "as" appears in the beginning of the definition: "A brand is created "as" people make an emotional connection..." This word is carefully chosen to reflect the dynamic process that is at work in a product or service becoming a brand. It does not happen overnight. It is an evolution. It can be nudged, cajoled, protected, nourished and fed, but it cannot be managed in the ordinary sense of the word, because the people who begin to make the transformation are customers, not company employees!

Have you ever seen curling during the Winter Olympics? The players do not manage or control the stone. They start it in the right direction at the right speed as best they can and then they nudge, urge, cajole and sweep it with a broom toward the spot in the "house" where they want it to go. It is an almost perfect metaphor for how executives must construe their powers and their job of caring for their brands.

A brand can be directed, nudged and nourished, but the belief that it can be managed ignores that the most important people in the world take over almost immediately and become the driving force in the process. These people are consumers and customers! Executives become servants of the people when they realize how brands work and how they grow. Why?

First, consumers and customers last forever. Presumably, if the brand is any good at all, the people who use it will become lifetime proponents or even raving fans. And, their children will "inherit" their brands. They have more longevity than the stewards of the brand inside the company who will leave, be promoted or retire.

The second reason that executives and managers should see themselves as servants of the people is that consumers and customers begin to imbue the brand with characteristics and expectations not necessarily found in the company's written strategy for the brand. This transformation demonstrates why we say a brand cannot literally be managed. Actually, a great brand can provide direction for the company that nurtures it. How can a brand direct you and your company rather than the other way around? The brand does it by communicating with you through brand language. Brand language comes from what your customers tell you about your brand. Quite literally, customers will tell you what to do to nourish your brand, but only if you listen very carefully. They will tell you how to grow the brand. Brands can do the managing themselves when executives take their cues from the brand language used by customers. For this reason the company must include customers' expectations for the brand in its strategic plans. If not, the customers will feel betrayed and the brand will languish.

Emotional Connection

The heart of a brand is wrapped up with how it makes people feel—how they feel while thinking about it, while dreaming about having it, while looking at it, while shopping for it, when taking it home for the first time, when experiencing it for the first time, while using it, while talking to other people about it, while other people are looking at it, etc. The feeling that they are seeking, usually without being consciously aware of what they are really looking for, is based on one or more of the many emotional needs we have identified through our research.

Transformation

As a product or service evolves, its brand gradually becomes more than its concrete attributes. It becomes more than the sum of its parts. The "more" that the brand becomes is the extra value that is being created. The extra value is the heart of the brand and that is what makes the brand the most valuable thing to any business.

Consider Starbucks. Starbucks is a coffee shop! Or is it? Of course it is, at least on a superficial level, but it is much more than that, at a deeper level. It is much more than a shop where one can pick up a quick cup of coffee. It is a great brand. Just look at how the stock price has performed over the past 15 years.

Everyone would agree, but try to articulate what there is about Starbucks that makes it a great brand. Doing so is not easy. The words come to the lips, but they do not always make a lot of sense. It is a struggle.

Go ahead now. Pause in your reading for a moment. Try to describe it. Try to explain it. Write it down.

Starbucks is a special place. Ah, the glorious aroma when you step into a Starbucks! There is magic in the experience, or it would not be enduring. But, it is difficult to articulate what makes Starbucks magical. Starbucks is an oasis that offers renewal and reward for people who are plagued by the demands of life. It is a part of the community, and allows people to gather, share ideas and forget about time and obligations. It gives people permission to take a break and relax. It also allows people to engage in a bit of self-indulgence, to spend time alone, engrossed in reading or work, while still being a part of the larger world around them.

You can see that Starbucks is much more than a place to buy coffee. The essence of the brand is rich and complex. The founders of Starbucks created a great brand using tacit knowledge and intuitive understanding of consumers. For a business to truly understand its brand, this tacit knowledge and understanding needs to be put into words. Without articulating the essence of the brand in this way, it cannot be communicated and the secrets of the brand are held forever in the minds and hearts of a few tenured employees. Whenever this happens, the understanding of the few is not communicated, and as the company grows, decisions are made further and further away from the core of what made the brand so great in the first place, and decline may set in.

As this book goes to press, Howard Schultz, the CEO who turned Starbucks into a global success has returned to the company to help it reconnect emotionally with its customer base. He had only been gone for a couple of years, but the company began to slow down. Why? Because he failed to articulate the secrets of the brand, so that they could be communicated to his successors.

Implicit Promise

Once customers begin to transform the literal product or service into something more than the sum of its parts, the magical personality or essence that makes it "more" begins to spread through word of mouth. The "more" is that little something that cues them that the brand can help them to feel the way that they want to feel. People begin to sense "the something more" on a tacit or implicit level. They intuit it or feel it, but do not overtly acknowledge it or articulate it. They are not yet consciously aware of all of the benefits of the brand, even though they are responding to the benefits and are motivated by them.

During this stage of the development of a brand, the product is not a great brand yet, but it is on its way to becoming so. It is gathering adherents who will go out of their way and pay extra to experience the feeling that it offers them. The foundation is in place for building a great brand. Much work needs to be done, but the brand is now on its way!

For years, the FedEx tag line was "Absolutely, Positively!" This tag line also represented the promise of the brand, which is what made it so powerful and motivating. But, the company drifted away from the theme line as it changed advertising agencies. The extent to which the creative execution of advertising leaves this tag line behind, the more this company puts its brand integrity at risk. A basic rule for all businesses is as follows: Do not change your brand promise or theme line just because you change advertising agencies. And, never change it so much that it communicates a rational message or even a different emotionally based message, if the current one is resonating with people.

Expectations

As time goes on and people talk to one another about the brand, they begin to articulate some of the benefits they are feeling when they buy and use it. As they do, the implicit promise comes closer to expectations that are more explicit and more easily communicated. People start to look for certain things when they encounter the brand. Above all they expect to feel a certain way at any of its touch points. The expectations are all of the little things that people look for in the brand. They look for some of them consciously as though relying on a checklist (left brain), and they look for others intuitively, driven by how they feel (right brain). They cannot put it all into words now. Indeed, they may never be able to put all of it into words, but they will know for sure when the brand lets them down. They will know when it does not come through for them and when it betrays them.

And, they will tell others about their disappointments.

Great brands just do a better job than their competitors of fulfilling people's expectations and delivering the emotional benefits that motivate them to be in the category in the first place. They differentiate themselves and emerge from the rest of the pack by delivering the emotional benefits a little better than their competitors.

This lesson is a difficult one for most marketers to grasp. They often ask us to find an attribute that they can own. Many times this is possible, but many times it is not a matter of owning an attribute, certainly not a product related attribute. Often it is a matter of articulating a deep-seated emotional need first and then sticking to it, hammering it into the minds of consumers and delivering on the promise in the marketplace so that the competition cannot encroach on the space that the brand owns in the mind.

Often having a different (and deeper) understanding of what consumers really want and knowing how to give it to them is more important than having a different product or attribute that can be owned. After all, FedEx, DHL, UPS and the US Post Office all provide an overnight delivery service, but FedEx shows people how they will feel reassured and have peace of mind if they choose FedEx to ship overnight. FedEx does not own an attribute, but it does own these emotional benefits in people's minds.

When you go back to work, think Starbucks. Think FedEx. Think about how the success of these brands is based on delivering emotional benefits, not just product attributes. Then think about what your brand can do to appeal to one or more of your customers' deep-seated emotional needs.

CHAPTER THREE

❯⊷❍⊶❮

Positioning

"If you can, be first. If you can't be first, create a new
category in which you can be first."

— AL RIES & JACK TROUT

Jack Trout and Al Ries have given marketers a wonderful gift. It is
a little book published in 1981, titled *Positioning: The Battle for Your
Mind*. In it they delineate their definition of positioning with such
clarity and force that we have made the book required reading in our
Consumer Psychology Training Program.

Trout and Ries define positioning as "a brand's claim to unique territory inside the consumer's mind." Clearly, their definition is different
from the more common use of the term. For example, an executive
might say, "Our company is well positioned for the challenges of the
twenty-first century." Or a marketing director might say, "Our product is well positioned in the five dollar and up shelf category."

Instead of focusing on the position that an executive thinks his
company or his product has established, Trout and Ries focus on what
the company or the brand means to the consumer. And, of course,
they zero in on the unique meaning of the brand or company—what
makes it different from all its competitors—in the CONSUMER'S
mind. Trout and Ries assert that it makes no difference how manage-

ment perceives the brand. For example, management might believe that the company's brand has a classy image and appeals to a need for prestige, but if consumers perceive the brand as having a sporty image, that is the only thing that is important. According to Trout and Ries the only thing that counts is what is in the hearts and minds of consumers in the marketplace.

Stop for a moment and think about what Trout and Ries are saying. It is a profoundly different perspective from the one that many CEOs and the members of their executive teams bring naturally to their businesses. They all bring an analytic lens to their businesses — a lens that focuses on the business. But Trout and Ries are saying that the primary focus should always be on the people who buy or might buy the products and services the business offers.

Now consider this: Trout and Ries use the term consumer rather than the word "customer." For them, a brand's position depends on what the brand means to everyone who is aware of it — not just what it means to people who buy it. The right word is "consumer," because in order for management's marketing strategy to grow the business, the brand has to have the same meaning for people who use it (customers) as it does for the people who management hopes will use it (consumers in the target market).

A brand carries with it a lot of imagery, meaning and associations. Some of it is crucial to understanding the core of the brand. Some of it is not. Some of it sets the brand apart from all other brands, which is its position in the minds of the consumers. The position is just one dimension of the brand. But, it is the most crucial part of it. It is what the brand stands for that differentiates it from other brands; it is created and defined by consumers, not the marketers.

A position provides instant recognition of the brand and instantly communicates the benefits of the brand. Without a strong position, the brand is reduced to a purely left brain price/value tradeoff. The value of a position is that it gives people a reason to buy; in a word, it is MOTIVATING. But what drives motivation? Fortunately, we know the answer: **emotion drives motivation**. The best positions, then, are those that have powerful emotional components — establishing links between the brand and an emotional need in the right brain.

Some brands become successful almost from the day of their birth. Whether it is due to entrepreneurial genius, intuition or in-depth research, these cases are few and far between. FedEx and Starbucks are great examples. More recently My Space and Facebook have taken the marketplace by storm. But, for each of these examples, there are thousands of failures. These many failures teach us that instead of leaving the success of the brand and its positioning to trial and error, it is far better to uncover the emotional benefits. Then, the benefits can be communicated systematically through advertising and all aspects of the brand experience.

The emotional need at the core of a position is often a subconscious component. In the case of FedEx, most of its customers could not articulate the real reasons why they use FedEx instead of a competitor. That is because their motivation lies in the subconscious. Even though most people cannot articulate these reasons, they are close enough to the surface that most people recognize the reasons when someone else articulates them or when they are probed repeatedly in an in-depth interview.

Consider Prudential Life Insurance Company. It is impossible to think about Prudential without thinking of "A Piece of the Rock." But, no one wants a rock instead of a life insurance policy. That would be irrational. So, what does the position convey? What does it really mean to people? Here are just a few of the possibilities:

- Permanence
- Stability
- Solidity
- Security

Taken together these associations communicate an unconscious message: immortality and eternity. This message comes through to the life insurance prospect without conscious awareness, giving the Prudential salesman a competitive advantage over other life insurance companies.

Since 1972 we have conducted well over 60,000 in-depth psychological interviews with consumers. We have learned the steps for developing a brand that is effectively positioned. Here they are:

1. Stake out the territory in the mind that no other brand claims using emotional research.

2. In advertising, appeal to the right brain with rich visual imagery.

3. Address an emotional need that is <u>NOT</u> emphasized by the competition. If this is not possible, then the brand must do a better job of addressing the emotional needs that motivate people to buy than any of its competitors.

4. Focus on motivation rather than description of the product.

5. Focus on the consumer rather than the brand.

6. Hammer the message into the mind repeatedly.

7. Direct all strategy and communication by starting with the position.

What brands can you think of that are clearly positioned in the consumer's mind? There are lots of them: Hershey, Disney, IBM, Kodak, Google, FedEx and Ivory Soap are all excellent examples. If you follow these seven steps, then your brand can live on and thrive like Ivory Soap has since 1879.

You will find it useful to stop here for a moment and make up a grid with the names of these iconic brands as well as any other brands that come to mind that have clear positions across the top horizontally and the seven criteria listed vertically in the left hand margin. Then rate each of these brands on a five-point scale representing how well you think each one has done in meeting each criterion. When you have finished this little exercise, you will find it illuminating to add several of your favorite brands. Then add the brand or brands that you nurture in your work. Once you have taken these three steps, ask yourself the following questions:

- How well are my favorite brands doing?
- How well are my brands doing compared to these icons?
- What insights can I draw from this exercise?
- What steps can I take to strengthen my brands?

Positioning is one of the secrets to effective marketing. And the secret to positioning is understanding the mind of the consumer and the emotional benefits the consumer is seeking. Positioning is necessary for success, but it is not sufficient. To be successful, you have to get the positioning of your brand right. Your brand has to be in alignment with what is in the consumer's mind. Great marketers and great brands need proper positioning to achieve and sustain greatness. No marketing campaign succeeds without proper positioning. No brand endures without it.

CHAPTER FOUR

>—•>—◦—<•—<

The Arkansas Test:
Ozark Mountain Wisdom

"He who refuses to embrace a unique opportunity loses the
prize as surely as if he had failed."

—WILLIAM JAMES

As you look at your brand's advertising, do you see a message that
would work just as well for another brand? Or, even worse, do you see
something that could also work in another product category?

Years ago Pete Herschend introduced us to The Arkansas Test. It
goes like this: If you place a Missouri State Tourism ad next to an
Arkansas State Tourism ad and they look alike, you are in trouble. If
they are interchangeable—such that all you would have to do is switch
the tag lines and the state names, then you fail The Arkansas Test.

Arkansas and Missouri share the Ozarks and often compete for
the claim on the Ozarks in people's minds. We know from the way
positioning works that two brands cannot simultaneously make the
same claim and both be equally successful. One brand—in this case
one state—will clearly win out over the other. Or, people will be confused. Confusion leads to inaction, which in the marketplace means
that both brands will suffer.

Of course, it was our client's experience with advertising that failed to stand out that moved him to develop The Arkansas Test. He began to use the test consistently whenever he evaluated creative executions. The emphasis he placed on the importance of differentiating one state, one brand or one product from all their competitors was always a key factor in the success of any campaign that he directed.

The challenge for Arkansas and Missouri is the same as the challenge for toothpaste, foot powder, hair spray and many other products and services. They all have similar product features and may even have the same product benefits. So, how do their marketers differentiate these products from their competitors?

There is only one way. It is to uncover the motivation to buy a particular brand or product at an emotional level. Once this discovery is made, the communication strategy can be built around showing customers that the brand or product delivers the emotional benefits that they are seeking. Marketers need to determine what consumers are looking for emotionally when they are choosing a product in their category. For example, are they seeking impulse control, escape, sex appeal, prestige…? And, how do consumers feel when the benefits they are seeking are delivered? Once the emotional motivation is discovered, it is a short step to develop creative executions that show consumers how the brand can deliver the emotional benefits they seek.

Over the years, our experience tells us that marketers who show people that their brands deliver the emotional benefits consumers are seeking will increase market share and profits the most. In short, the best way to pass The Arkansas Test is to demonstrate that a product or brand meets the key emotional needs driving the category. Marketers need to seize the moment. They need to embrace the opportunity to stake out unique territory whenever it presents itself, for when they do not take action, the competition surely will.

Today, many commercials start out by showing the opposite of the emotional benefits sought by consumers. Then, after wasting 20 or even 25 invaluable seconds, the scene shifts to the brand coming to the rescue, but by this time the advertiser has already done unwitting damage to the brand. The way the mind works is that viewers associate the negative scenes they are shown first with the brand, a fact of life that creates just the opposite effect from what the advertiser intends. The net result is that many brands are unwittingly eviscerating the equity that they have already established in people's minds!

The right way to develop your communication strategy is straightforward. Avoid negatives. Avoid the competition. Avoid campaigns driven purely by creative. Avoid the latest fad. Instead, figure out how your brand makes people feel and then tell the world! And, do not waste any money telling the world anything else.

PART II

HOW? THE RIGHT BRAIN WAY

CHAPTER FIVE

>—•—0—•—<

Right Brain and Left Brain

"There is a beauty, a synergy, an interconnectedness, an
absolute overpowering aspect to the natural world,
which I think leads you to the divine."
— PETER GARRETT

In this chapter, we explore in depth the differences between the right
brain and the left brain, how they work and what these differences
mean for executives who make strategic decisions about their brands.

Understanding the brain and how the mind works starts with the
simple fact that we all have two brains: the left hemisphere and the
right hemisphere connected by the corpus callosum. The corpus callosum consists of approximately seven billion neural fibers. Electrical
impulses pass back and forth across these neural fibers, making it possible for the brain to function as one entity even though there are two
brains: the left brain and the right brain.

In the 1940s and 1950s, Wilder Penfield, a Canadian neurologist
and the Director of the Montreal Institute of Neurology, conducted
his famous work focusing on people with epilepsy. When he stim-
ulated the surface of the brain of an epileptic patient with an electrode, much to his amazement, his subjects saw experiences from their
past in vivid detail, as though they were looking at videotapes of the

events in their mind's eye. This phenomenon is often referred to as the Proustian "flashback" effect. Penfield concluded that all human experience is stored in the brain in its original form and that people's memories can be accessed with the right techniques.

Then, in an attempt to reduce his patients' seizures, Penfield administered a local anesthesia and probed the patient's brain tissue while the patient was conscious. He used this technique to locate the damaged brain tissue causing the seizures. While using this technique to cure epileptic seizures, Penfield was also able to map areas of the brain and their related functions. He found that the right brain is visually oriented and recognizes pictures but not words, while the left brain recognizes words but not pictures. When information enters the mind in pictures, it will remain there as long as there is sufficient energy or emotion attached to the experience. For this reason we say that the left brain communicates in words and language, while the right brain communicates in pictures.

Penfield's work led us to the realization that we could access the right brain through pictures—picture memories so to speak. Relying on Penfield's understanding of how the mind works, we developed a methodology which taps into the right brain and allows respondents to relive experiences they have had with a product or a brand.

Even the brain has a limited capacity. It cannot store pictures based on every experience that people have. Emotion provides the sorting mechanism. The more emotion that is attached to an experience, the more energy is generated and the more likely it will be that a picture based on this experience is stored permanently in long-term memory.

Since Penfield's research in the 1950s, we have known that the right side of the brain, or right hemisphere, houses emotions, creativity, motivation and long-term memory. For this reason accessing the right hemisphere of the brain allows us to uncover the emotional needs and barriers that drive the way people feel, their decisions and their behavior. And, this model applies to everyone in all kinds of situations:

consumers, voters, clients, customers, employees, business associates, friends, family members, etc.

What makes an otherwise conservative 55 year-old grandfather who is near retirement purchase a brand new red Corvette? We find that Corvette owners are a distinct breed. They all have one thing in common: they are seeking to recapture a bit of that special feeling of exuberance when they were young, carefree and without responsibility. In right brain terms, they are looking for rejuvenation and renewal. These consumers are fulfilling an emotional need by choosing a Corvette over a Cadillac or a Lexus.

In order to understand the emotional motivators that drive these decisions, it is essential to access the right brain. Tapping into the emotional motivators housed in the right brain allows us to answer "why" questions. As we have seen, the answers to "why" questions provide organizations with strategic direction for growth and success.

Long before Penfield's work led to the definition of right brain functions, Paul Broca made the first scientific discovery of the localization of brain functions. His patient had suffered a brain injury while working on the railroad. The injury to the left hemisphere had left him unable to speak. Moreover, speech therapy proved to be useless and Broca soon realized that his patient would suffer this disability for the rest of his life. Although Broca's work is more than 150 years old, his conclusions proved correct. Modern brain science honors his discovery by referring to the part of the left hemisphere that controls speech and language as Broca's Area.

Thanks to Broca, we know that the left hemisphere of the brain is the seat of logic, language and reasoning for behavior that is driven by the right side of the brain. It is also the location where short-term memories and conscious awareness are stored. The left brain acts to balance, control and explain actions that are driven by emotional needs seated in the right brain. All human behavior is an interplay of the left and right brain—a beautiful and synergistic interconnectedness.

These discoveries by Penfield and Broca give us the scientific foundation for our unique brand of emotional research—The Right Brain Approach.

Most IQ tests measure left brain skills such as mathematics, inferential logic, abstract thinking and verbal skills. These are also the skills focused on in formal education. The further one moves through the educational system, the greater the emphasis on left brain skills and the more one is rewarded for developing these skills to the detriment of right brain skills. Therefore, it is not surprising that most business leaders and decision makers are more comfortable with apparently logical, often statistical, ways of analyzing and addressing business challenges. Unfortunately, focusing just on the left brain side of the equation misses half the picture of human behavior.

People naturally want to appear to be logical and rational. Therefore, they will always explain their reasons for decisions and behavior through rationalizations. Getting beyond these rationalizations to the real motivation for what people do is the key to understanding customers. Only by getting beyond rationalizations can one gather information on which to base strategic direction and decisions. This information can only be obtained through specially designed methodologies to capture right brain information.

On the surface consumers seem to be dominated by their left brains. For example, when consumers are comparing prices and making other rational decisions, the left brain is in play. But when they are making actual purchase decisions, they fall back to the emotionally rewarding and comfortable right brain motivations. They want what they want because of motivations that are based in the right brain.

Although much is made of the rational decision making process, most long-term behavior and decisions originate from the right side of the brain. It is the right brain that houses the long-term memories and emotional needs that drive consumer behavior and consumer decisions. The left hemisphere actually provides the logical sounding rationalizations that people create in order to justify their emotionally based decisions and impulses. They justify their decisions to themselves first and then to others!

When asking people why they choose to do business at a particular bank, they will first say that it is convenient and it offers the services that they need, when, in fact, those statements are most likely true of all banks. Such statements are rationalizations and as such are not the primary reason for their behavior.

In order to understand why people bank where they do, it is essential to understand the dynamics that drive the use of banks in the first place. People feel out of control when they put their money in a bank. They feel threatened that they may not be able to get their money when they need it. Therefore, they search for clues that will reassure them that their money is safe. And they want to feel that there are people at the bank who "know them." If there is a problem, they want to feel reassured that the bank will take care of the problem and in doing so, take care of them. The only way that they can really feel reassured is to "know" someone at the bank, someone who knows them and treats them with respect.

All of this sounds irrational and silly to most bankers, and for that reason, most banks do a poor job of providing prospects and customers with the reassurance that they seek. However, a few small banks have become highly profitable because the founder or the CEO has an intuitive understanding of these dynamics. Unfortunately, the large banks lost this connection with their customers a long time ago. In the wake of the sub prime fiasco of 2007, bank customers have come forward to tell how even the private banks in the offshore islands and in Singapore lost the feel for the customer amidst the mania for fees, corporate banking and asset based securitization.

Savvy marketers in other businesses know that understanding the emotional component gives them a complete understanding of why customers make the decisions they do and what the influencing factors are in their decisions. With this understanding these marketers are in an ideal position to give consumers good reasons "why" they should buy their products. Bankers could learn a great deal about how to treat customers by looking at how luxury brands are revolutionizing the retail space in Shanghai's Bund, Tokyo's Ginza and Hong Kong's Pacific Place. Brands such as Louis Vuitton, DeBeers LV and Chanel have made dramatic new investments in the highest rent districts to introduce unprecedented new levels of service, privacy and comfort for their shoppers.

Information about what people really want is invaluable because it provides an edge in today's competitive market—an edge that will impact and change customer behavior. It also makes it possible to position brands strategically in the minds of customers.

Understanding how the right brain and left brain work is crucial to any situation in which people have perceptions, feelings and make decisions. Insight into emotional motivation is invaluable for answering a wide variety of questions about consumer behavior, business-to-business relationships, employee morale, corporate mission and even in the non-profit and public service world.

Understanding how the mind works guides everything we do for our clients. Whether seeking the answer to a strategic or a tactical question, it is imperative to understand the structure and organization of the mind. This understanding drives how we conduct our interviews, how we analyze our interview material, how we report it to our clients and how we work with them to develop powerful brand strategies.

CHAPTER SIX

>—·—0—<·—<

How Right Brain Research Works

"Intuition will tell the thinking mind where to look next."

— JONAS SALK

"Eighty percent of our life is emotion, and only 20 percent
is intellect. I am much more interested in how you feel than
how you think. I can change how you think, but how you
feel is something deeper and stronger, and it's something
that's inside you."

— FRANK LUNTZ

The right brain is the seat of emotion. We must access the right brain
if we wish to understand the emotional needs that shape how consumers feel about the purchase of goods and services. We access the right
brain by having respondents close their eyes and view the "pictures"
in their minds of experiences they have had with different products
and services. The pictures that respondents see in their minds' eyes
are emotionally significant to them. The pictures are available to them
because the emotion they experienced at the time locked the visual
images into their long-term memories. Once respondents are viewing
past experiences with the product or the service, we interview them
about what they are seeing and how they are feeling in the picture.

This technique elicits information that is much richer and far more revealing than information produced from more traditional interview methods, because people are actually reliving the experiences they have had in the past and are in touch with the feelings that are associated with those events.

In 2002 the ad agency for a major pharmaceutical firm was looking for some breakthrough methods for their client's new product development process. The ad agency recommended to the company that they conduct emotional research. We met the people on the marketing team. Much to the surprise of their agency, the brand team told us that they were already doing "emotional research." Then they showed us the methodology. It consisted of the traditional seven and ten point Likert scales with "happy faces" and "sad faces" at opposite ends of the scales instead of numbers or words. It would be nice if such business challenges could be addressed using this type of kindergarten iconography! Unfortunately, solving problems in the world of business is never that easy.

Even serious market research fails to get at the emotional level in respondents' minds. For example, in the traditional market research interview, the interviewer might ask a consumer, "Why did you go to that restaurant?" The answer will always be shaped by rationalizations and posturing, preventing the interviewer from accessing the real reasons for the consumer's behavior and decision-making. To circumvent rationalizations and posturing, our method allows respondents to forget that they are being interviewed as they revisit emotionally significant experiences. Instead of giving us information filtered by judgments of what is proper or what they think we might want to hear, our indirect approach is designed to encourage them to tell us about their experiences in a way that reveals what really motivates them.

Since 1972 we have uncovered 47 emotional needs and 24 emotional barriers that drive consumer behavior. We have organized and defined these needs and barriers into a classification system, or taxonomy, which assists us in the analysis process. Then, when working for a client for the first time, we uncover the needs and barriers that work in the client's category and for the client's brand.

Our taxonomy gives us a framework for understanding how people's minds work. After the interviews are complete, we identify the key emotional needs and barriers that shape respondents' feelings and drive their behavior. Then we move to analyzing the findings for similarities across respondents, which allows us to understand the emotional motivators that drive consumer behavior in a particular category.

Based on this understanding of what motivates consumers in the client's category, we develop implications for the client's business and specific recommendations that will serve as a cornerstone for overall business and marketing strategies, including the following:

- Sales
- Promotions
- New product development
- Brand strategies
- Advertising
- Web site development
- Customer satisfaction
- Customer service
- Public relations
- Décor

Emotional research is a powerful tool for understanding consumers, because it provides the deepest level of psychological analysis possible. Executives and managers at all levels within the enterprise are able to use the emotional research results to answer questions about marketing and new product development that arise over time, including many that had not been anticipated prior to the research.

The findings and insights generated by emotional research excite the imagination, provide strategic direction and live on for years after we conduct the research.

CHAPTER SEVEN

>⊳─◇─⊲◄

How the Subconscious Mind Works

"Half the money I spend on advertising is wasted; the
trouble is, I don't know which half."

— JOHN WANAMAKER, FATHER OF THE DEPARTMENT
STORE

How the Subconscious Mind Works Through Pictures

Remember Wilder Penfield, the Canadian neurosurgeon, who worked
with patients with epilepsy by stimulating certain parts of their brains
with an electrode? In this process, he found that his patients recalled
scenes from their childhood in vivid detail. They always recalled these
scenes in pictures, like a dream. It was as if certain brain cells contained definitive experiences from the past, and each time he stimu-
lated a different area of the brain he would get a different picture or
scenario from the past.

For many years scientists had been searching for the elusive engram—which is the physical location in the brain of a specific memory.
To this day this work is the closest scientists have come to connecting
memory traces or picture memories to specific physical locations in
the human brain.

Discovering the engram as Penfield did raises an important question for marketers: Does the mind store everything like a security camera? No, for that is probably beyond its capacity. Even security cameras have to dump the tapes from their hard drives on a regular basis. The mind does, however, store many emotionally based events from the first five years of life—which most people do not remember without help. These events are stored in the subconscious mind and can be retrieved with hypnosis or with other methods. Such memories are not easily recalled, but they can be recalled by evoking a person's "picture memory."

What does this discovery of how the mind works mean for business, and especially for marketing and advertising? Consider measures of advertising recall. An advertising message or a commercial may have a high recall score, but that does not mean that it is effective in doing its job. It does not mean that it motivates the people who see it. The commercial could be funny or absurd, making it easily recalled, but if it is not connected to the brand or does not key into an emotional need, then it will not motivate people to act. On the other hand a message may go into the subconscious part of the mind and serve as a permanent motivator, even though there is no immediate recall of the message.

In other words, a message can motivate behavior without the person realizing it. Typically, when market researchers ask for recall, they are tapping into the consumer's conscious mind. When we ask for recall in Right Brain Research, we ask for it in pictures, and as a result we get much truer and richer information about what motivates people. There are two reasons for the rich information that we can attain. First, we are tapping into a different part of the consumer's brain—into the right brain rather than the left brain. Second, the right brain is the seat of emotion and third, we are bypassing the rationalizations people give to justify their decisions.

This insight into how the pictures of the mind work provides the psychological understanding that explains John Wanamaker's dictum about wasting half of his advertising dollars. If Wanamaker had only known which half was working effectively for him, he could have doubled his success.

Photographic Memory

Some people say, "I once knew someone who had a photographic memory, and boy was he smart!" Very few people have a photographic memory for everything, for that is very rare, but the fact is that nearly everyone has a photographic memory for some things. The trick is to know how to use it. When information enters the mind in pictures, it will remain there as long as there is sufficient energy or emotion attached to the experience. In these cases the information is locked into the mind and may be recalled many years later with some help as long as the person does not suffer memory loss from dementia.

Many people report having had a déjà vu experience whereby they are overcome by the feeling of having been in the same place before. Yogi Berra has done us the favor of popularizing the déjà vu phenomenon when he talked about having a déjà vu experience all over again! This strong feeling follows the visually based experience of going somewhere that feels familiar in some way as though one has actually been there before; the experience can be very powerful and overwhelming. People often become uncomfortable about this experience when they cannot make the connection to a similar place that they have visited. Their discomfort demonstrates that memories go into the subconscious and often resist recovery.

In working to develop a methodology that could be used to answer Pete Herschend's "why" questions regarding Silver Dollar City, we discovered that by having people visualize the experiences they had had at the City, we were able to get them to tell us all sorts of things they could not tell us otherwise. In this way we learned to ask "why" questions in pictures, rather than by asking the questions directly in words or in thoughts. This discovery opened up a whole new way of researching consumer motivation.

People do not have an unlimited capacity for recall, even when asked to use their picture memories. They can picture things and experiences that stand out for them when asked to do so. The pictures form rather quickly and they can describe these pictures in great detail. They can visualize things in the pictures that have an emotional charge. When they first have these experiences, the emotion that is attached to them provides the energy for the pictures to circulate among nerve connections in the brain sufficiently so that the pictures are locked into specific brain cells. This phenomenon explains the well-known fact that older people suffering from dementia forget some things and remember others in seemingly haphazard patterns. The explanation is that brain cells are dying and as they die, the locked-in visually based memories die with those brain cells.

Unlimited Storage Capacity

The subconscious mind sometimes seems to be a bottomless pit. There seems to be no limit to the amount of information that can be stored there. Certainly there is a limit, but we have not yet found a product category, no matter how mundane it may seem to be, that people cannot tell us about based on long "forgotten" experiences that are buried in the subconscious.

From shortening to computer software, from mascara to motorcycles and from mustard to imported salami, people can go back in their minds' eyes and see early experiences with the product or service. Depending on the product category, they readily go back to age four, five, six or seven. The significance of these early experiences is that they often lay down a template for the person's behavior for a lifetime of consumer decisions.

Deaths, love affairs, operations, departures, rituals such as weddings, funerals and graduations—all of these kinds of events are easily recalled, because of the emotion associated with them. Some emotionally based events are buried in the subconscious, subject to recall only through pictures. But they can be recalled.

One of our favorite projects delved into the Psychological Dynamics driving the selection of engagement rings. When we begin a Right Brain Interview, we always make sure that our respondents are actually seeing something in their minds' eyes. In this case, we asked our respondents to look at the salesperson in their minds' eyes and tell us what she or he looks like. Almost instantaneously our respondents began to tell us very specific details about the salespersons' appearance, including details about the jewelry they wore. The finely grained details confirm for us that they are actually seeing a picture in their minds' eyes.

For men who had bought a ring for their fiancées recently, clear and detailed memories may not be surprising, but the surprise is that the clarity and detail of the descriptions bore no relationship to the length of time it had been since the respondents' buying experience. Some of our respondents had been married for thirty and thirty-five years—yet their pictures were just as clear as the pictures in the minds of the younger men.

The conscious mind cannot possibly process all of the information in the environment. Much of this information passes through to the subconscious, unprocessed, and stays there. So, the subconscious also serves as a passive receptacle for "extra" input or overload—even if it is not apparent that emotion is attached to it.

Let us use the restaurant business as an example. In traditional interviews and focus groups we find that many people are unable to give us their reactions to the décor in a restaurant because they "forgot" or "did not notice it the last time they were in there." However, when we ask for the same information in "pictures" it pours right out of their subconscious minds. People see a lot more than they would ever imagine. When the information pours out, they can tell us about the colors, shapes, artwork and structure of a dining room. They tell us about the foreground and the background.

For business purposes, tapping into feelings in this way can give us a new level of information. People tell us what it is about the cues that make them feel the way they do. They can connect their feelings to specific cues in the environment, and they can use their imaginations to change a cue and tell us how the changes impact them emotionally. These kinds of results allow management to understand what it is about the décor that is working for them at the emotional level, what is not working and why. It allows them to see how they should refine and improve the décor to make a positive psychological impact on their customers. And it allows them to predict the impact of their decisions on customers.

No Dimension of Time

Subconscious processing is not subject to the restraints of time. Past, present and future are mixed together in the subconscious mind. Can you imagine for a minute how you would negotiate your day if your conscious thought processes were not structured by time? We can look to dreams for an idea of what it might be like. Everyone has had the experience of dreaming about a present event or activity that becomes confused and intertwined with events from the distant past. Since all dreams (even daydreams) arise from the subconscious mind, this phenomenon indicates that linear time is missing in the subconscious.

The fact that linear time is not present in the subconscious has many implications, several of which are extremely important for business purposes. First, an experience or event that happened many years ago can still be buried in the subconscious mind. Although the person may not be able to describe the event consciously, the emotion associated with it may still be present. Sometimes pictures will just "pop up" in the mind, unexplained, simply because an emotionally charged event that is taking place in real time is associated in the person's subconscious with something similar from the distant past. This type of experience is called a "triggering event," because it releases the emotion connected to a long "forgotten" experience. The emotion may flood over a person, disorienting him temporarily or perhaps making him anxious, even though he is unaware of the cause.

Some years ago we had a client who was working on a line extension of a well-known brand of analgesics. We had recruited respondents who complained of a "sick headache," a loosely defined condition that is less serious than a migraine, but with some of the same symptoms—headache accompanied by nausea. One respondent, a 64 year-old man, took us back to his senior year in high school when he was headed out of the house with his basketball grip in tow to play in the state championship game. He told us that just as he opened the front door, his mother shouted out, "Now don't miss any foul shots!" He told us that he stopped dead in his tracks at that moment, as he was instantly overcome by a pain in his head accompanied by a sharp pain in his belly. Ever since then, whenever he finds himself in a particularly stressful situation, he suffers a sudden attack of a sick headache similar in form to the first one. Yet, he had never connected his life long suffering from sick headaches to the original event—not until the Right Brain Interview!

We call the original experience the "initial sensitizing event." Then, later in life, other things happen that bear an emotional similarity to the sensitizing event. These events are called triggering events when they evoke the same or similar emotional reaction.

Many products and brands succeed because they are part of the initial sensitizing event and then later they serve to evoke a similar emotional reaction as part of a triggering event. Corvettes have this kind of power. In one interview that we conducted, a respondent recounts that as a 14 year-old freshman in high school, he was transfixed by a recent graduate from his own high school who had just gotten his first job and was able to buy a Corvette. Our respondent was impressed that this guy had essentially purchased a 4,000 pound girl magnet. So, he told himself that guys with Corvettes are successful with the girls. Then, later in life, when he is feeling a bit harried and begins to feel that he may be losing that youthful sense of being carefree, he panics and buys a Corvette without even realizing on a conscious level why he is doing it.

The second implication of the irrelevance of time is that the subconscious mind cannot accept a beginning or an end to life. Since there is no concept of linear time in the subconscious, there is no beginning or end. This is the most important implication of all, for it leads to the most important human need in any need hierarchy: the need for a long, long life—in fact, it is the need for unending life! Since time is absent in the subconscious mind, the mind will not accept the fact that life comes to an end. This discovery gives us an enormous advantage when it comes to explaining all human motivation, because the need surfaces in a wide variety of products and services.

Throughout history man has sought secret formulas, magic potions and hidden places that could give him the precious gift of immortality. We all know about Ponce de Leon and his search for the mythical Fountain of Youth in the Sixteenth Century. There are many others who have devoted their lives to this unending search. Our work demonstrates that this quest, which has beset every generation of man for thousands of years, originates in the subconscious mind. We also know that the quest is recapitulated in everyone.

Of course, people accept logically and consciously the fact that they will not live forever, but emotionally, they just cannot accept it. So, most people believe in some form of afterlife or life without end. Not surprising, all of the world's religions are dedicated to the belief that life will not end.

One does not have to look very far in order to see that people will use their ingenuity to invent all kinds of ways other than religion to extend their lives and make themselves immortal. Immortality can be achieved through movies, books, inventions, work, families, civic and social groups and fraternal and religious organizations. There are about as many ways to achieve immortality as there are people!

We have interviewed many respondents who attempt to immortalize themselves through their work. One respondent had made millions in the computer business, and although his health was bad and he was in his late sixties, he woke up at 4:00 AM five days a week, in order to drive to distant cities to see clients and to attend business and computer fairs. When asked what it is that drives him, his answer was simple: "greed." But greed is not the answer; greed is the rationalization. The real answer is that he was looking for immortality in his work by establishing a legacy that he could leave behind. One does not have to look very far to see people who are doing the same thing.

Ironically, people say "You can't take it with you!" But most people deep down do not really want to take it with them. What they want to do is leave it behind them. They want to leave it behind in a way that it will memorialize them forever! The "it" is not money; it is legacy.

Many businesses are built on the premise of unending life and the need for legacy. One very good example is the gigantic financial services industry called life insurance. It is often thought of as a product that people buy for others, but in the emotional mind, no one ever buys anything for other people. They are buying the emotional benefits for themselves, even if someone else will benefit from the literal product or service.

In the insurance industry, one often overlooked motivator for buying is that people want to do the right thing. They want to feel that they are people of good character. They will buy a product that can never benefit them financially, just so they will be remembered as good providers who wisely took care of their families by buying life insurance. In this way, they leave a legacy and feel that they can live forever through their families whose members remember them and the wise decisions they made as good and responsible providers.

The third implication of the lack of linear time in the subconscious is that people can readily go backwards in time in their dreams and in their fantasies. In fact, the subconscious is drawn to experiences and images that represent simple and less complicated times often in the past. Theme parks and historical exhibits that recreate the past are popular attractions. And inside businesses, we often hear about the "way things are done here" in such a way as to imply that doing them in any other way would bring down the "wrath of the gods" as well as the wrath of the CEO!

In the late 1970s the King Tut exhibit drew record crowds when it came to the United States, and no one was able to explain why. Think about it for a moment. Tut, the Boy King, had achieved a kind of unending life. He had achieved immortality to an unprecedented extent. Four thousand years after his death, he is available for people to look at. No wonder people flocked to the exhibit!

Now in 2007 and 2008 King Tut is back again. A much larger, much more powerful exhibit is touring the country as we write these words. The King's message is one of immortality. Recently, they have removed the sarcophagus and revealed his face for the entire world to see. He continues to draw attention and publicity. The message never dies and the King never dies!

There is another King who will never die. Yes, he is the King of Rock and Roll, the one and only Elvis. In 2007, President Bush and Prime Minister Koziumi visited Graceland in my hometown of Memphis. The visit realized a lifetime dream for the Japanese Prime Minister! He amazed everyone with his singing (he has cut a CD of his favorite Elvis songs) and his excitement over the King. Forty years after The King's death the head of a government half way across the world is fulfilled beyond measure by visiting Elvis' home and his grave. Now, that is a legacy!

WHAT THE SUBCONSCIOUS MIND DOES

The Subconscious Mind Feels Rather than Thinks

The subconscious mind is the storehouse of emotion and also the center of human motivation. People act on the basis of their feelings. They take action because something makes them feel a certain way, not because of reason or logic. When certain feelings are triggered, a person acts. Love, hate, anger, desire and fulfillment are all words that people attach to feelings that are stored in the subconscious.

Victims of strokes to the left side of the brain are left without the ability to talk, but they can still utter vulgarities and obscenities! This fact never ceases to amaze those who take care of them, for such words are the only ones that they can utter. Of course, such words are closely attached to emotion and that explains why they can utter these words and phrases, for the source of emotion is in the healthy part of their brains—the right brain.

A Sense of Timing

The subconscious mind does have a sense of timing. It does not keep track of time the way a clock does, but it can sense the time of day. Many people complain that they wake up early even on days when they do not have to go to work—often at exactly the same time each day, or just before the alarm clock is set to ring. Most business people can get up on time without relying on a wake-up call, just by giving themselves the suggestion that they need to wake up at a specific time in the morning.

Dogs are like humans in that they have an intuitive sense of timing. The family dog often seems to "know" when the school children are coming home. Many dogs in rural areas run loose all day long, but are always there to meet the children at the school bus on time. Others become suddenly alert just before the master or mistress arrives home in the evening. These behaviors reflect an intuitive sense of timing, not the ability to "tell" time.

ACCESSING THE SUBCONSCIOUS MIND
Through Repetition

Advertising relies on repetition. The psychological defenses surrounding the subconscious mind are tough, and they are designed to protect survival functions.

Repetition is necessary to penetrate these defenses. Repetition is exactly what brainwashing is all about. The effectiveness is based upon unending patience on the part of the brainwasher.

Repetition in advertising today is very expensive and it is also becoming less and less effective. Broadcast TV no longer dominates the airwaves. While few people were looking, in 2005 cable TV surpassed broadcast TV in total ad revenue. The implications of these developments are only gradually sinking in. As a result most brands still depend far too much on the expensive and wasteful methods of 20 years ago.

John Wanamaker's quote about wasting half of his money on advertising is apropos here. Today, we believe that it is even worse. Most companies waste 80% to 90% of their advertising dollars. Why do we say they waste 80% to 90% of their investment? The reason is that most advertising is not based on an understanding of how the brand connects emotionally with the consumer.

The trick is to get the message right, before costly production begins. You get the message right by understanding what motivates people. If you hit their hot buttons square on, you can have greater impact with fewer repetitions and fewer dollars. If you know what motivates people to buy, if the campaign is based on this knowledge, if the execution is right, one exposure to a consumer should be sufficient to impact that consumer on an emotional level. What a revolutionary idea!

THE SUBCONSCIOUS MIND IS CONCERNED WITH SURVIVAL

The subconscious mind readily receives suggestions that support beliefs and ideas it already holds. This phenomenon makes a lot of sense, since it only holds beliefs that are necessary for survival. Therefore, when marketers say things to people that are consistent with their ideas of survival, it is easier to circumvent consumer defenses and have them accept what is being said. This is why patriotism is a popular subject with almost everyone, for if America survives, we all survive. A patriotic speech is still very popular. The audience experiences goose bumps and often cheers. The more the speaker says what they already agree with, the more they like it.

The subconscious mind is programmed for survival. Part of the function of the subconscious mind is to provide continuity for the vital physical functions, such as respiration and heart rate, which are involuntary and automatic. These are some of the physical survival functions.

The instinct to survive is with people at birth. Breathing and sucking are reflexes that are already programmed into the subconscious mind and help us to survive. And within the subconscious mind, survival is paramount throughout life.

The well-known case of Terri Schiavo (she suffered brain damage and became dependent on a feeding tube, living for some 15 years in that state) illustrates how the subconscious mind will continue to act in the interest of an individual's survival even though there may be little or no conscious will to survive.

The Schiavo case illustrates the concern of the subconscious mind with physical survival. At the time of birth, physical survival is the major issue. Later on in life, as development occurs, the subconscious mind begins to manage three other major survival functions, which we shall describe in Chapter 11 on the Taxonomy of Emotional Needs and Barriers.

The subconscious never accepts a suggestion that is contrary to an individual's survival. For example, there has always been a question as to whether or not a hypnotist could successfully put a suggestion in a person's subconscious to kill himself or to kill someone else. The answer is that the subconscious will simply not accept such a suggestion, because it conflicts with the survival instinct.

Some people argue that the massacre at Jonestown, Guyana in November 1978 disproves this assertion about survival. But if anything, the Jonestown story actually supports these observations. The people at Jonestown took their own lives, voluntarily, because they were told that their spiritual survival was dependent upon it. Since spiritual survival—or unending life—is more important than physical survival, there are many cases in which people willingly end their own lives in preference to losing their souls.

Since 9/11 we have become aware that terrorists and homicide bombers advancing the agenda for the Islamo-Fascists are motivated at least in part by the promise of carnal pleasures in the afterlife. They are motivated by a kind of spiritual survival that causes them to give up their physical lives in return for a promise of everlasting bliss.

The subconscious mind allows a person to smoke, drink or perform other dangerous activities which seem to undermine his survival. The reason is that the subconscious has been programmed, at some time in the individual's lifetime, to associate smoking or drinking with survival. That is one of the reasons why it is so hard to stop these activities, once they are started. People smoke and drink because they feel—subconsciously—that they must engage in these activities in order to survive. This is true even though they have been given conscious and rational information, which says that these activities are bad for their survival. The reason that this rational information does not work in the effort to change their minds is because it impacts the conscious mind, rather than the subconscious mind.

THE SUBCONSCIOUS MIND IS THE SEAT OF CREATIVITY

Experts agree that creativity consists of bringing together two previously divergent and disjointed ideas into one. These diverse and disjointed ideas are believed to be in the subconscious mind, often for many years. The subconscious is like a giant warehouse with limitless storage, filled with many ideas that might never even be used. But every now and then, two of these diverse ideas will come together and create something entirely novel and unique. This dynamic is what we call creativity.

THE DIFFERENCE BETWEEN THE SUBCONSCIOUS AND CONSCIOUS MINDS

Communication with the subconscious is quite different than communication with the conscious mind. This point is critical for advertising and marketing efforts. Communication should be aimed primarily at the subconscious mind, not at the conscious mind, because consumer decisions are based upon emotion, not reason. Reason supports emotionally driven desires and impulses, but it is not the source of them.

People are driven to want a product, a service or a brand by the emotional needs in their right brains. They justify their decisions and rationalize them in their left brains. The key for marketers is that the origin of the desire for products and brands is lodged in the subconscious, the right side of the brain!

The goal of advertising is to convince people. The reason for knowing how the mind works is to improve the process of convincing people. We believe that knowledge of the subconscious is imperative in order to communicate with people and to persuade them effectively. Convincing people depends primarily on having the right message. It does not depend primarily on repeating it over and over again. Moreover, repetition of a message that is off target is not only wasteful, but can be counterproductive, causing what we call the Boomerang Effect.

The Boomerang Effect occurs when a message or commercial actually has the opposite effect from what is intended and damages the brand rather than building it. The metaphor is based on the idea that time and effort spent sending the wrong message does not impact consumers; instead, it comes back and hits the marketer in the forehead, giving him a massive headache, just like a boomerang.

So now that we know about the left brain, the right brain and the subconscious mind, how do we use all of this knowledge to accomplish our goal of understanding genuine consumer motivation?

CHAPTER EIGHT

>-◄►-◊-◄►-◄

Visualization: The Royal Road
to Human Emotions

"It's surprising how much of memory is built around things
unnoticed at the time."
— BARBARA KINGSOLVER

In the mid 1970s, we MADE a simple but vital discovery. We found
that when we asked people to close their eyes, then guided their visual imagery and asked them to tell us about the details of the visual
pictures in their mind's eye, we were able to access information richer
and more substantive than information gathered from other more traditional methodologies. This discovery became the cornerstone upon
which we developed The Right Brain Approach.

The Right Brain interview technique that is based on this discovery is visualization. Why is visualization so important? Visualization
unlocks people's memories. Here is how it works. When an experience
has an emotional impact, the emotion stamps a visual impression of
the experience into the mind. It is emotional energy that activates a
place in the brain for this particular picture to be stored. The human
brain—even in its nearly infinite capacity—cannot store everything
that we experience. Functionally then, the human brain has evolved
and adapted using emotion as the mechanism to determine which

70

information will be stored in the mind. Emotion signals what is important. The brain listens and stores it as visual impressions. Visualization opens the door to the details of these stored pictures. Here are the seven logical steps beginning with a "why" question and ending with the need for the visual technique:

The Logical Path Linking WHY Questions to Visualization
1. The marketer asks the question: Why do they buy?
2. "Why" questions about behavior can only be answered by studying motivation.
3. Motivation is driven by emotion—emotional needs to be specific.
4. Emotion is located in the right brain.
5. To get at motivation and the emotional needs that underlie it, we need to access the right brain.
6. The right brain communicates in pictures—it is visually oriented.
7. Therefore, we need a visual technique for interviewing people. That technique is visualization, which we use to allow people to relive their experiences with a product, brand or service.

These steps provide the rationale for using visualization as an interview technique. Visualization is an integral part of the Right Brain Approach.

How do we know that the information we evoke in people when they close their eyes is important (i.e., based on emotion) and not just random? The best example—good now only for people born before 1958 or so—is the Kennedy assassination. Everyone—without exception—who was old enough to be in school in 1963 can see in his mind's eye where he was, who was there, who told him and how he felt! The shock and the intense emotion account for the clarity of the details. We have interviewed many people about this awful day. At the time of the assassination, they were in grade school—many of them in first or second grade. As we are interviewing them, they can actually see the clock on the wall in their classroom. Many say that it reads a few minutes after one o'clock as the teacher is telling them the news of the shooting.

Now consider this question: How many people have equally clear picture memories of the five days that followed the day that the President was shot? Not many! Why not? Because the immediacy of the shock was over. In the following days they were in a depressed state and as a result their memories are blurred together in their minds. Many people remember Jack Ruby shooting Lee Harvey Oswald, but do not remember anything else that happened during these five days until the funeral, from which they have clear images of the riderless horse, Jackie Kennedy, Caroline and John John's salute.

I have used this example myself nearly 1,000 times in speeches, meetings and training sessions. When I do, I see (even with my eyes open) myself sitting with my friends in the graduate student lounge at Clark University. And then I see Paul Werme coming over to us and telling us that the President had been shot! Now, Paul was a friend—but not a really close one—and we lost touch with one another after graduate school. I never think about him or see him in my mind's eye unless I am telling this story. I need to evoke the image in my mind's eye before the information about who was with me and how I really felt is available to me. This is how a Right Brain Interview works—whether it is about beer, furniture, cars, software, shortening, motorcycles or mascara.

For those readers who are in their thirties, the Challenger disaster or the assassination attempts on President Reagan or Pope John Paul II may be salient. But, they are not universally present in people's minds, because the shock value of these events and the consequent emotional trauma is not comparable to the Kennedy assassination.

But if you ask people where they were and what they were doing on September 11, 2001, they can provide intimate details as to where they were, who they were with, what they were doing, how they felt about what was happening on that awful day, what they said and who they called. They recall colors, faces and articles of clothing. The pictures in their mind's eye are almost as clear to them as the day that it happened.

There are many life experiences that have enough emotion surrounding them to stamp the experiences firmly into the mind so that years later when they are evoked you can see them in your mind's eye—almost like reliving them. Some of the ones that come to mind that you may identify with are:

- Your graduation day
- The death of a loved one
- An automobile accident
- The death of a pet
- Moving day—into a new house
- Moving day—into a new office
- The day you met your spouse
- A sporting event of special importance to you
- The time you met a famous person
- The first time you drove a new car
- The moment you arrived in a new country for the first time

Now, you may say that these events far outweigh the mundane shopping experiences for soap and toothpaste, beer and soda, mascara and perfume. Surely they do, but we find that there does not need to be earth-shaking emotion attached to a purchase or the use of a product for visual images to be firmly stamped into the mind and then later to be accessible through visualization. In fact, we are constantly amazed by the degree of emotional intensity that underlies buying and using a wide variety of everyday products and brands. Examples of some products that may appear to most readers to be mundane or "low involvement" categories, which actually carry plenty of emotion with them, include:

- Analgesics
- Fragrance
- Rice
- Shortening
- Insect repellant
- Pet food
- Deodorant

We find that emotion is involved in the purchase and use of these products, as it is with all products. The trick is to understand the two basic elements, logic and emotion, and how they work together to drive consumers to do what they do and feel the way they do about your product, your brand or the competition.

CHAPTER NINE

>━▷━◦━◁━◈

Listening: The Suspension of Belief

"Oh wad some Power the giftie gie us
To see oursels as ithers see us!
It wad frae monie a blunder free us
An foolish notion..."
("Oh, would some Power give us the gift
To see ourselves as others see us
It would from many a blunder free us,
And foolish notions...")

— ROBERT BURNS *To a Louse*

Why do businesses conduct qualitative research and why do they conduct quantitative research? In general they conduct quantitative research to measure things that they already know about. For most kinds of quantitative research, the basic nature of consumer perceptions, brand attributes, product dimensions and buying predispositions are incorporated into the questionnaire at the outset. The purpose of most quantitative research is to measure prevalence, frequency, intensity of things that they are already aware of. And, then the secondary purpose is to find differences among groups of consumers. Therefore, most quantitative research is not designed primarily to discover anything new.

Qualitative research is entirely different. One of the primary objectives of qualitative research is to be surprised. Consumers may say something that is entirely new. Or, at least, managers may discover that something previously known to them that they had not thought to be terribly important is actually much more important to consumers than they had realized.

Given that surprise is one of the primary objectives of qualitative research, then what could be more important than approaching the research with an open mind? We call this approach "suspension of belief" and it is a necessary step to encourage surprises to emerge. It is the foundation, the *sine qua non*, of qualitative research.

Yet too often marketers enter the observation room looking for things that will confirm their preconceived ideas. Marketers succumb to the unspoken desire that their customers be just like them, or that they fit a previously constructed mold. Time and time again, we hear our clients tell us that they want the baby boomers, the yuppies or the upscale consumers. Of course they are saying that they want people just like them as their customers. It is rare indeed to hear marketers say that they want to move down the socio-economic ladder and increase their penetration of the blue collar or working class market.

This mindset makes selective listening inevitable. It is easy for the things that respondents say that support these preconceived ideas to be "heard" and remembered, while the things that contradict these ideas are not noticed or are explained away. People are generally not aware of the extent to which their expectations can influence what they hear and how they hear it. Conventional wisdom, "the way things are done here," prevailing paradigms and existing assumptions all too often guide and affect the listening process.

In 1973 when Americans were panicking in the middle of the first Arab oil crisis, consumers screamed long and loud about the "outrageous" gas prices at the pump. The Big Three felt threatened and hurriedly conducted research to find out what people were saying. Of course they heard a lot of emotionally charged accusations, conspiratorial theories and outrage. They tried to respond by changing the messages in their advertising. All of a sudden the American public heard car companies like Oldsmobile touting the wonderful gas mileage delivered by their cars.

What is the lesson here? Marketers can learn a great deal from the demise of this great American icon and the brand blunders that caused it. Oldsmobile left its brand equity behind and shifted gears from being a luxury brand with new technology to becoming a brand of smaller cars with good gas mileage. As a tactical move, this shift may have made sense in the very short run, but the company abandoned its new technology platform and moved so far away from its heritage that when the crisis subsided, Oldsmobile "forgot" what had made the brand the fourth largest car company in America and continued to promote good gas mileage. The next 15 years saw one failed campaign after another, culminating in one of the worst brand blunders in history: "It's not your father's Oldsmobile."

Simply put marketers at Oldsmobile and elsewhere assumed that the overriding outrage over fuel economy was the consumer's primary motivation. They carried these assumptions with them through their research efforts and let these same assumptions dictate their advertising and messaging strategies for reaching the consumer. They confused the consumer's temporary preoccupation with fuel economy with what really motivates people over the long run to buy new cars, to prefer one brand over another and especially to buy an Oldsmobile.

If they had been able to acknowledge fuel economy as an issue while listening to their customers' messages with open minds and if they had been able to suspend belief, they would have found that some of the excitement and magic surrounding Oldsmobile was still alive in the minds and hearts of customers and those aspiring to own one. We were able to uncover the excitement and magic as late as 1990, even though by that time it had faded quite a bit. Imagine how powerful the Oldsmobile brand must have been in 1973 and 1974 given that there were still vestiges of its magic in the early 1990s! In the early '70s, Oldsmobile had been the fourth largest selling brand in the business. In 2004 the last Oldsmobile rolled off the assembly line in Lansing. A brand that Americans used to sing a song about died unnecessarily.

We emphasize the suspension of belief when our clients join us in the field to observe Right Brain Interviews. Their experience is very different from observing focus groups or other one-on-ones. Everything we do is aimed at understanding the real motivations for why people do what they do, why they make the consumer decisions that they make, why they believe what they believe and why they react the way they do to a variety of marketing messages.

We find that the more closely they listen, the less they talk to one another and the more they focus on respondents, the easier it is for them to suspend belief and to leave themselves open for real surprises. We find that when they approach the research with an "open ear," they hear things that they have heard before, but now they hear them in a different light and realize that they have a meaning and an importance that they had not recognized previously.

The insights and discoveries that come from our interviews fall into three categories. First, there are some things that our clients already know. Then, there are some things that are complete surprises. Finally, some of the most powerful insights that we uncover fall into the category of "tacit knowledge." Thanks to the inspiration provided by Michael Polanyi (1891—1976), Professor of Social Sciences at the University of Manchester, tacit knowledge is best described as knowledge that is felt or intuited but never clearly identified or articulated. All marketers have intuitive knowledge of their brands and their customers. All marketers use this knowledge to some degree. All marketers secretly want to use it more, but do not know how to use it because they do not know there are methodologies for doing so. When clients suspend belief and truly listen, they hear things that they may have wondered about or suspected, but never heard out loud. With Right

Brain Research, for the first time, this knowledge is expressed in words and it is expressed in the very words their customers use.

Articulating tacit knowledge about their customers and about their business is often one of the most powerful things that Right Brain Research brings to its clients. The reason is that tacit knowledge is of little use in business unless there is just one person making all the decisions. Tacit knowledge by definition cannot be communicated, so no matter how rich the insights, without being able to communicate them to other members of management, the knowledge is left untouched as an island unto itself. Right Brain Research brings life and words to this tacit knowledge and makes it possible for people in business to discuss what they feel, know, think they know and intuit about their market.

People who observe one-on-ones and focus groups should always suspend their own beliefs and start with the respondents' perceptions. Suspension of belief is built on the premise that searching for objective reality is irrelevant. Instead, what is important is how respondents perceive and construct their own "reality" and where and how and why the product, service or brand fits into that reality. We look to Robert Burns, the Scottish poet and Renaissance man, as our inspiration, for it is to him that we owe the modern aphorism that "Perception is reality."

To see a product, a brand or a service as a consumer sees it is a powerful gift. It is also a simple concept, but it depends on suspension of belief and in-depth analysis of qualitative information.

CHAPTER TEN

>─◦─◦─◦─◦─<

What Respondents Say:
The First Step of Analysis

"The lady doth protest too much."
— WILLIAM SHAKESPEARE, HAMLET

Recall the movie *The Last Picture Show*. On the surface it was about the closing of the last movie theater in a small Texas town. On a deeper level it was about identity crisis, growing up and the conflicts teenagers experience over the direction their lives may take. I keep waiting for someone to write the book: *The Last Focus Group*. Focus groups are a long-running fad like the small town movie theater. How long can they last? Everyone in business complains about them, but much like the weather, no one ever seems to do anything about them!

People complain about focus groups for many reasons. Perhaps the biggest problem with groups and the way they are used and misused today is that they encourage observers to commit the cardinal sin of research, which is to take what people say at face value.

Now if you believe that people know exactly why they do what they do and if you also believe that they are going to tell you exactly why in front of strangers, then you are no doubt happy with your research methods. On the other hand, if you believe that people are not or cannot be completely forthcoming about their decisions in the marketplace, then you are reading the right book. You are in the right place to discover new and exciting ways to conduct qualitative research so that you do not expose yourself to the risks of focus groups. The following table provides a complete comparison of Right Brain Research and focus groups:

DIFFERENCES BETWEEN RIGHT BRAIN RESEARCH AND FOCUS GROUPS

RIGHT BRAIN RESEARCH	FOCUS GROUPS
One-on-one interviews	Group sessions
Ideal for buying decisions made by individual consumers	Ideal for buying decisions made by groups of consumers
Psychological Approach	Sociological Approach
In-depth methodology	Comparatively superficial approach
At least three analysts	Usually just one "moderator"
Team approach to analysis	Usually just the moderator conducts analysis/often client receives transcripts only
Built-in controls to prevent subjectivity	No controls for subjectivity
Interviewer controls interview	Group members usually allowed to control the group
Results are consistent/form a pattern	Results often differ from group to group
Visualization accesses consumer emotions	Verbalization restricts access to emotions
Repetition of questioning to circumvent consumers' defenses	Repetition of questions would be too obvious
Relaxation exercise lowers consumers' defenses at beginning of interviews	Presence of others heightens consumers' defenses
75 to 90 minutes of emotional information per respondent	10/12 minutes of information about opinions per respondent

RIGHT BRAIN RESEARCH	FOCUS GROUPS
Focus on real reasons people do things	Focus on rationalizations people give for behavior
Respondent cannot "fool" interviewer	Respondent often "fools" himself and group leader
Social pressure to conform is minimized	Social pressure to conform is maximized
Respondents not influenced by other respondents	"Opinion Leaders" can contaminate an entire group

BELOW THE SURFACE: WHAT PEOPLE SAY VS. WHAT PEOPLE MEAN

When people ask me what we do, I tell them we figure out why people buy things. I also tell them that we specialize in NOT taking what people say at face value. Uncovering what people really mean, rather than just focusing on what they say, requires sharply developed listening skills.

Here is an example of what a respondent says and the analysis of what he really means. It is a verbatim that illustrates some of the subtleties of how language works in the process of analyzing a Right Brain Interview:

I bought the TV at Macy's. I felt I wouldn't find it <u>drastically cheaper</u> somewhere else.

Earlier in the interview, this respondent said cost is the most important factor for him in selecting a television set. Now he is saying that he felt he could get it cheaper elsewhere, not that he bought it at Macy's because this store had the best price or even a good price!

Here, we see a contradiction that deserves thorough probing. In this respondent's mind, cost may mean something other than the cheapest available. We might ask the respondent, "As you look at this picture in your mind's eye, what is telling you to get it here, even though it is not the cheapest price?" As we probe further, we find that shopping at Macy's means something special to this respondent. It is a place where he often sees friends and leaders in the community and a place where he is often seen by friends. The old families in town shop at Macy's and there is a certain status about it. All in all, he trades off price for less tangible, but more intense emotionally-based benefits that are connected to the shopping experience, not to the TV itself.

In this vignette we see an example of how people do not actually do what they do for the reasons that they think they do. Hence, they cannot tell us directly why they do what they do. In order to get this information, we need a methodology that is designed to access the part of the mind that the respondents do not ordinarily have access to. Right Brain Research is the methodology that accesses the emotional mind and allows us to find out why people do what they do.

In banking research, and in all research involving retail stores, "convenience" is always one of the first words out of the mouths of respondents. If we look at the dictionary definition of convenience we see the following:

- Being near at hand
- Convenient for use

If we take what people say at face value, then we would assume that just as is the case in the real estate business, "location, location, location," "convenience, convenience, convenience" is the end all and be all for banking customers. However, when we are in our first visualization with a respondent and he tells us he uses Bank One because it is convenient, yet he describes walking past Bank of America to get to Bank One, which is two blocks further away from his office than Bank of America, then there is much more going on than convenience as it is normally understood in everyday language. In fact, when we probe further with this respondent, we find out what is really going on in his heart of hearts:

- Less wait time in teller lines
- Better treatment by the tellers
- Someone who knows him by name
- A banker who can make a decision without keeping him waiting
- A place he trusts

With this background it is not surprising that he actually knows one of the platform people personally at Bank One, whereas, he does not know anyone at Bank of America! Convenience, then, actually has nothing to do with physical proximity for him. Instead, when he talks about convenience, what he actually means is something different. It is not convenient to know people at the bank, but it is very reassuring. It is reassuring to be able to feel that his money is well taken care of and that he will be taken care of as well.

Once again, taking what people say at face value is misleading and dangerous.

We tell clients to pay very careful attention when respondents "deny" that something they are mentioning is a negative for them. Usually if they say something like, "It's not that this bothers me," it means that it really does bother them. Why? Well, our analyst did not ask directly if it bothers the respondent. The respondent raised the issue. The respondent is protesting too much like Shakespeare's character in *Hamlet*. Therefore, we regard the Old Bard as one of the fathers of consumer psychology!

When a respondent volunteers that "It is not that I feel bitter toward them for doing that to me ten years ago" we know for certain that she does indeed feel bitter toward them, because we did not introduce the word "bitter" into the interview. She did! She mentioned it and then denied that it defines how she feels.

The Right Brain Interview: Getting at the Truth
People cannot tell others all of the reasons that they do what they do

using conventional conversation. The Right Brain Methodology addresses this simple fact by stripping away opinions, rationalizations and "face-saving" statements to get at respondents' real motivators. The three core Right Brain Interview techniques are relaxation, visualization and repetition.

The Right Brain methodology takes respondents into a very relaxed state, with their eyes closed. They wear masks that block out the light — masks just like the ones that can be found at cosmetics counters and on transoceanic flights. We call it a visualization mask.

We use visual techniques in conducting Right Brain Interviews so that we can answer "why" questions that the respondents probably could not answer without the benefit of the interview. The first part of the interview is a visualization exercise. This exercise, in which they picture a time when they are at home feeling very comfortable, is designed to relax respondents but, more importantly, it is designed to "teach them" how the rest of the interview will work.

Then, we ask respondents to visualize real experiences they have had that relate to the brands, products and questions that our client wants to hear about. We direct them to these visualizations with carefully worded requests that limit them to the information we are seeking, but still allow them to self-select episodes that are really important to them. They will see themselves having these experiences, which is a little bit like watching themselves in a movie, but it is more than that because they are actually in the movie as they relive it. And, they will "relive" these experiences, telling us about what is happening to them, what is going through their minds as it is happening and how they are feeling as the pictures get clear.

Respondents often use the present tense as they respond to the analysts' questions. When they do this, it is an excellent sign that they are having highly concentrated and very vivid experiences. They are truly reliving the experience in their mind's eye.

We have a specific set of objectives in mind when we start each interview. It is necessary to control the respondent in order to achieve these objectives. As clients observe the interviews, they see an emphasis on probing rather than on sensitivity. After all, it is not a clinical interview. We are not trying to help our respondents. Instead, we need to get them to help us!

Once respondents are relaxed and visualizing experiences with a brand, product or service, we use repetition to draw out details from their experiences and to uncover insights into the real motivations that underlie their surface, more rational answers. Looking for specific information, analysts ask respondents the same questions several times in several different ways. Other times, an analyst may use a different type of probe or questioning tack to get specific information from the respondent.

Our typical interview lasts about 75-90 minutes. It may seem that this is a very long time, but respondents frequently say something like, "What, already?" when told that the time is up and they can take the mask off and blink their eyes to get them readjusted to the light. When they are deeply reliving right brain experiences, their awareness of the passage of time fades.

We tell our clients that they may hear things that they disagree with or things that are painful to listen to, but that whatever respondents tell us in these interviews is much more direct and reflective of how they really feel about their products and brands than they will hear with other methodologies. Keep in mind that the name of the client and even what questions are to be answered are kept from the respondents. Respondents have never been through an experience like this before, and so they are a bit disoriented, which is good for us. Respondents do not know what we are after, so they do not know how to alter their stories, in order to please or frustrate us. The Right Brain Methodology allows our clients to gain pure insight into the minds of their customers by uncovering both positive and negative feelings about their brands. But, to hear the truth about a brand, the brand team has to suspend belief and listen closely in ways that they have not done before.

Most respondents work very hard at being rational and controlled. Most will open up gradually over the course of the interview rather than all at once. Sometimes they will react and show emotion as they tell us about what is happening, but they often show emotionality indirectly by using metaphors and similes, by pausing or by altering typical word usage slightly in very subtle ways.

We watch for body language that signals defensiveness or a lack of defensiveness. Sometimes, the key to what is really going on underneath the surface is seen in their body language.

We listen for contradictions in what the respondents are telling us in different parts of the interview—it often means that we are accessing an area of emotional significance. Whenever people contradict themselves there is an underlying dynamic that explains what is happening—often outside of their conscious awareness.

The Danger of Taking Things at Face Value

The Coca-Cola Company committed the all-time brand blunder by taking things at face value. Pepsi-Cola had been stealing market share to the point that the new executive team decided that they had to take drastic action. Coca-Cola's market share had dipped from 24.3% in 1980 to 21.8% in 1984. So, in April of 1985, the company announced plans for a product called "New Coke."

The formulation for New Coke was based on a $10,000,000 investment in blind taste tests, all of which "proved" that people preferred Pepsi to Coke. Surprisingly, Coke drinkers preferred Pepsi too. There was no difference between the two segments of customers in their preference for Pepsi (when they did not know what they were drinking) in all of the blind tests conducted.

Then Coca-Cola gave them a new drink that was sweeter, much more like the Pepsi formulation. Overwhelmingly, consumers preferred the sweeter Coke formula to the traditional Coke formula.

Shortly thereafter Coca-Cola launched New Coke with the most fanfare of any new product introduction in history. Within weeks the Coke executive team began to realize that they had made a terrible mistake. Millions of people called and wrote to the company to complain bitterly. Consumers organized public demonstrations and boycotts. Nationwide, people said that the company was taking something away from them and that they had no right to do it. A retired Air Force officer wrote to Coca-Cola executives, explaining that he had planned to be interred with a can of Coke, but that he had changed his mind because of the change in the formula. The outrage was unprecedented. Amazingly, consumers were wildly indignant about the change in the formula of a carbonated beverage!

What went wrong? Coca-Cola executives had been looking at what people told them and took it at face value. Never did they explore the underlying emotional connection to the brand. They did not appreciate what a great job they had done over the previous one hundred years in creating the brand and hammering it into the heads of consumers. Coke had become the great American icon, but the executives at the company did not realize it, nor did they realize the implications of changing the brand—even in an attempt to improve it.

Documentaries of the story of New Coke show people talking about their feelings for Coke and how much they detested the new product. These interviews by reporters reveal much more than the taste tests and focus groups conducted by Coca-Cola. They uncover some of the deeper-seated emotion that Coke had come to evoke in Americans. But how did the people at the company miss what was under the surface? They overspent on study after study designed to prove themselves "right," but never spent a cent to find out if the change in formula was perceived by their loyal customers as fitting with the Coke brand. They conducted a lot of left brain research, but they did not conduct any emotional research. They may have understood their product, but they certainly did not understand their brand!

Once New Coke became a corporate disaster, Coca-Cola set out to make lemonade out of the lemon they had created with their blunder. Incredibly, their recovery strategy worked so well that some pundits began to suspect that Coca-Cola had planned the entire episode as a publicity stunt. This paranoid conspiracy theory evaporated as news of the background that led up to the decision to launch New Coke leaked out.

The most parsimonious explanation for how a smart, experienced person like Roberto Goizueta, the Chairman of Coca-Cola at the time, could preside over such a blunder is the best one and the only one: Coca-Cola listened to what people said and never asked the right questions that would have allowed them to see the big picture. They committed the cardinal sin of consumer research. They took what people said at face value. They never looked below the surface and they never looked back until it was too late.

The Benefit of Digging Deeper

In the first projects we conducted for Saturn in 1986 and 1987, no one actually told us directly that they wanted an integrated, holistic, one-stop fits all experience that would allay their deepest fears about being abused and ripped off in a car dealership. Instead, we found subtle contradictions, little cues and other suggestions that needed further research.

Twenty years after we conducted our very first project for Saturn, I can still picture a female respondent who had "crossed the Rubicon," as it were, from domestic brand territory into the land of the imports. A life long buyer of domestic brands, she had become so disgusted with the frequency and cost of repairs that she broke down and finally bought a "rice burner." (A rice burner is a derogatory term from the 1970s and 1980s meaning cheap Japanese import. It is a tribute to the

Japanese and Asian brands that this term is no longer in common usage.) Then five minutes later in the interview she told us about how the engine in her sister-in-law's Toyota had literally dropped out of the car while it was moving along the freeway!

> Julius Caesar was part of the Triumvirate, consisting of three leaders of the Roman Republic who had worked out a power sharing agreement. Each leader had his own army and his own territory. The arrangement was tenuous. Tension and disagreements boiled over and the Republic was on the verge of civil war. Based in Gaul, Caesar marched south and hesitated at the Rubicon River, a small stream in Northern Italy that served as the southern border of his territory. He contemplated crossing the Rubicon, but hesitated because he knew that once he did, his action would be irreversible, he would plunge the Republic into civil war and the Republic itself would be in danger. Finally, seeing no other alternative, he and his troops crossed the Rubicon, crossing from his territory into enemy territory, effectively declaring war on the other two leaders and changing history forever.

Needless to say we were shocked at the contradiction. In this case she was never able to provide an explanation, even when confronted with her lack of logic. Instead, we heard some elaborate rationalizations about how this sorry event was an exception, etc. She had invested so much energy in making the transition to the imports that there was no way that she could ever go back to the domestic brands again. She actually felt that she had betrayed her country, a territorial survival issue, when she bought her first import brand. It was painful and difficult for her to do, but she did it because she had felt that her physical survival was threatened by her unreliable car that kept breaking down.

In our hierarchy of emotional needs, we know that physical survival is more basic than territorial survival. When the two conflict with one another, people nearly always elect physical survival. Think for a moment about all of the dictators who have abdicated and run into hiding as the revolutionary horde storms the palace. When people are conflicted between trying to stay in power and staying alive the choice is obvious. They elect to stay alive.

Finding the Patterns: Analysis Continued...

Sometimes we arrive at insights about what respondents' language actually means during the interviews, but more often it is during the week of formal analysis after the interviews when the interpretations of people's words begin to emerge.

"Emerge" is an important word for describing the process of analyzing Right Brain Research material. In many cases none of the respondents actually spell out in explicit terms what is really going on underneath the surface and even more importantly what it all means for the business and for the brand. In these projects the analysis focuses on what people mean and how they really feel, rather than what they say. Here is another example.

Product Development Case Study—The Right Brain Difference

Ken Kring is a client of The Right Brain People and is the developer of Kring Strategy Mapping. The hallmark of the Kring approach is to depict a company's business challenges in a visual format. The method lays out the steps that are necessary to address the client's challenges so that they can be read and followed like a road map. A portion of Kring's strategy mapping process encourages business leaders to understand the strategic importance of emotional motivators and to support them throughout the company's product development, marketing, operations and finance functions. Hence, Kring Strategic Mapping is not only a powerful marketing tool, but also a strategic tool for the entire business.

When talking about the emotional needs of consumers, Kring uses the word "uncover" because he has found that emotional needs must be revealed instead of stated. In focus groups, the stated needs shared by participants are often misleading or sometimes just wrong. Henry Ford understood this when he quipped, "If I had asked people what they wanted, they would have said, 'Faster horses.'"

One of Kring's career changing experiences occurred when a focus group research project produced misleading results for him. He was working for a credit card company on a new product introduction—a time saving "go pass" that attaches to a key ring. Kring says, "As we worked through the new product concept, some consumers stated in focus groups that they would not use the new product because they felt it would get lost or be stolen. However, when we asked these same consumers about the traditional credit cards they were using, they conceded that their wallets could be lost or stolen even more easily than the 'go pass.' So why had they rejected the new product? Something was not adding up. We needed to understand what was really going on. We needed to get at something we couldn't simply ask them about."

Kring came to The Right Brain People for a deeper understanding of the contradiction these consumers expressed. Kring says, "In the Right Brain interviews, consumers told us their stories from pictures in their minds' eyes. They did not know what the 'right answer' was supposed to be. The Right Brain Approach uncovered the hidden emotional drivers that shaped consumers' feelings about our new product. Uncovering the real needs and barriers helped us understand the contradictions we had heard in the focus groups. The key finding was that consumers did not trust themselves with the new product. They did not trust their ability to control their impulses to spend. People were afraid they would overuse the new product because it was so convenient to use. It triggered their fear of losing control. Because they were unable to admit their subconscious fear, they rationalized their rejection of the product by saying they were afraid of losing it or having it stolen. If they really were afraid of losing a 'go pass' or having it stolen, they would be equally afraid of losing a traditional credit card or having it stolen, and they would leave their credit cards at home. That is why it was clear to us that the fear they stated in the focus groups was a rationalization and not the real fear that they had. By unmasking the underlying dynamics driving the statements respondents had made in focus groups, we were able to see why they rejected the card."

According to Kring, understanding what was really going on in the minds of consumers shaped his company's product development, marketing, operations and finance functions. For example, product development added a cover to the "go pass" to protect it from view as well as a disconnect mechanism to allow keys to be given to a valet. In terms of marketing, the "convenience" message was toned down to reduce the anxiety of potential customers who were concerned about losing control of their spending. Operationally, the fulfillment processes and the packaging were changed to boost security. These modifications led to a refinement in the financial models for the product. Following the recommendations that arose from the Right Brain Research positively impacted how Kring's company introduced the product and ultimately led to more sales than had been previously projected. The product was later praised by *Business Week* and *USA Today* as one of the "best new products of the year."

Kring says that making good business decisions requires understanding consumer behavior and allowing it to direct the product development, marketing, operations and finance functions. To achieve this goal, you need to begin by uncovering *what is really going on* in the hearts and minds of the consumer. For Kring, this is where The Right Brain Approach has been incredibly valuable. Kring's story is a wonderful illustration of how Right Brain Research fits into the overall business enterprise by providing new insights that reveal critical consumer motivations. And it demonstrates that solid emotional research affects all facets of the corporate enterprise.

There is always much depth and richness of information below the surface of what people say. It is vital to look for the underlying dynamics that are not immediately obvious during the analysis process. Our taxonomy is the most important tool we use as we conduct the analysis and look for the underlying dynamics.

CHAPTER ELEVEN

>⋅⟶⋅⟶⟨⋅⟩⟵⋅⟵⋅<

The Right Brain Taxonomy

"Science is the systematic classification of experience."
— GEORGE H. LEWES

As our client in the previous chapter noted, in order to understand consumer behavior, you need to begin by uncovering what is really going on in the hearts and minds of consumers. You cannot merely ask people directly what motivates them and expect their answers to provide a complete and accurate explanation. People's answers are driven by their desire to appear rational. They do not deliberately deceive researchers who ask direct questions about their motivations; rather, they are not consciously aware of why they do what they do. Therefore, they cannot verbalize the real reasons for their behavior when confronted with a direct approach. They explain their behavior with rationalizations that only give a partial explanation for their behavior.

Our indirect approach circumvents rationalizations and delves into the subconscious mind, uncovering rich emotional information that explains behavior. Once we uncover this information, then we must have a way to name, describe and define it in order to use it to make good business decisions. Our system for organizing the emotional information that we uncover in interviews is our Taxonomy of

Emotional Needs and Barriers. A taxonomy is a systematic methodology for distinguishing, ordering and naming types and groups of items within a subject field. Charles Darwin spent five years traveling the world conducting an exhaustive study of the varieties of plants and animals he observed. He classified them into Kingdom, Phylum, Class, Order, Family, Genus and Species—scientific terms used to categorize living beings into a hierarchy. Similar to Darwin's classification of plants and animals, our taxonomy categorizes human emotional needs and barriers as they influence consumers' decisions in the market place. Our taxonomy is the product of over 36 years of conducting consumer research. The taxonomy explains nearly all of what consumers do in the market place.

We find that marketers tend to focus too much on highlighting product attributes and do not focus enough on figuring out what motivates consumers to buy products. Motivation is explained by the emotional needs and barriers in people's minds that drive the way they perceive, feel, think about and behave toward a product. Emotional needs motivate people to do what they do. In advertising language, the term "hot button" is often used to refer to what motivates people. "Hot button" can be used as a synonym for emotional need. When we use the term "emotional need," we are referring to one of the 47 needs that we have uncovered over the years. Often, "hot button" is used to refer to something that is specific to a certain product category or brand. For example, a hot button for consumers who buy hand tissue might be "softness." When used in this way, the hot button is not a synonym for an emotional need. Emotional needs transcend specific product attributes. They are universal, not particular to a specific commercial or product. And they reside inside the mind of the consumer. When marketers fulfill one or more emotional needs of consumers with their products or brands, they can create a buying predisposition and ultimately a sale.

Emotional barriers block consumers from doing what the marketer wants, hopes and needs them to do, which is to "Buy my product!" There are 24 emotional barriers; they can be fears, worries, concerns or underlying conflicts. In many cases, sending a message to consumers so that it will register with them and motivate them to buy includes breaking through an emotional barrier or finding a way to "go around" the barrier.

The Taxonomy divides the 47 emotional needs and 24 emotional barriers into four psychological survival domains: physical survival, territorial survival, sexual survival and spiritual survival. People are driven to protect themselves in these four survival domains in order to feel complete and satisfied emotionally. Physical survival means that people are driven to maintain their physical well being by avoiding pain and harm and seeking pleasurable, restorative experiences. Territorial survival means that people are driven to protect the integrity of their property and to add to it. Sexual survival is about the need people have to express their sexual urges — impulses that assure the preservation of the species. People are also compelled to seek out ways to preserve their individuality during their lives and after their physical deaths, ensuring their spiritual survival.

Over the years, "Madison Avenue" has been accused in serious essays, books and exposés of appealing much too often and too strongly to sexual motives and to pairing brands and products with sexual imagery, even when it does not seem to fit the situation. We suggest that by overdoing the use of sexual imagery, marketers are missing opportunities to appeal to emotional needs that fall within the physical, territorial and spiritual survival domains.

We can best understand the way these four survival domains work to influence consumer behavior by looking at examples of several needs and barriers as they appear in the Taxonomy of Emotional Needs and Barriers.

SPIRITUAL SURVIVAL: NEEDS AND BARRIERS

Need for Character Maintenance: People want to feel that they are good people who do the right thing. When people are tempted to do something they perceive to be wrong, but choose instead to do what they perceive to be right, they feel good about themselves and feel that they have strong character. The need people have to feel that they are doing the right thing emerges in many different product categories. For example, in one project on specialty golf club grips, we learned that golfers perceive that the grips they choose reflect the type of people they are. They want the grips on their clubs to communicate that they are thoughtful, conscientious people who are serious about golf and, therefore, serious about life. They believe that having the right golf club grips allows them to express themselves as people of strong character, which they believe encourages others to take them more seriously than they otherwise would.

Need for Absolution: People want to feel that they can have their personal wrongdoings (or sins) forgiven or pardoned. Absolution allows people to start fresh, to have a blank slate and to have a clean conscience. Many women use bleach in their bathrooms and kitchens in an effort to make the countertops and surfaces clean, which they say makes them feel like they are starting anew. But they seek more than just a fresh start, because we find in their language that unconsciously, they are really concerned with purity. The extreme cleanliness they are achieving allows them to feel that they are starting anew emotionally, free from worry about character flaws.

Need for Escape: It is well known that people want to get away from everyday experiences. They want a break from where they work and where they live. The Need for Escape explains the frequency with which people take vacations, short getaways and long weekend trips. Providing people with escape experiences is perhaps a trillion dollar industry. But the Need for Escape is much more complex than it seems on the surface. People do not realize that when they seek an escape experience, they are actually trying to get away from themselves! They are trying to escape from their own inner conflicted feelings and anxieties. For example, on a project for a beverage company, we found that people slip away from the present and from their internal conflicts and anxieties when they enjoy refreshing beverages. One respondent, a book salesman who is not entirely happy with his job, escapes the sometimes frustrating routine of his work day by taking a break with a cool bottle of water under a Banyan tree before making a sales call. The label on the bottle reminds him of being in the mountains on vacation when he drank cool, fresh, mountain spring water. In the warmth of a Florida morning, the bottle of water gives him an escape experience as he revels in his fantasies and re-energizes himself.

Need for Rejuvenation: People are overcome periodically with the desire to be refreshed and renewed after a period of difficulty. This need is about wanting to feel young again, or to get a second wind in order to finish the day or finish a project with a feeling of satisfaction. In one project, we interviewed men and women in their fifties who feel that they are losing their edge at work. They get tired early in the afternoon and feel that their bodies are breaking down as they get older. They drink a nutritional beverage every afternoon to get a lift of energy and to keep their minds sharp as they complete their work day.

Fear of Judgment: People are afraid that they will be judged harshly by others if they do the wrong thing or make a poor decision. People want to feel that they act appropriately, but sometimes there is a fine line between their perception of what is appropriate and what is inappropriate behavior. For example, on a project for an organic food company, respondents said that there is a point at which consuming too many organic products would make them appear fanatical to their families and friends. However, to use too few organic products would make them feel like people who do not take proper care of themselves.

The fear of being judged as fanatical is a barrier to respondents increasing the number of organic products they buy.

Fear of Loss of Impulse Control: People fear that their impulses to do socially unacceptable things will spin out of control. They fear that they could eat or drink too much or spend too much money. We see this fear operating as both a motivator and a barrier in the cookie category. While working for a company that markets a premium brand of imported cookies, we found that their customers avoid buying "cheap" cookies out of a fear that they will eat too many of them and ruin their health in the process. This fear that they will lose control of their impulses motivates them to buy a premium brand. They keep these more expensive cookies for themselves and do not share them with their families. They only allow themselves to have two or three cookies each day with a special drink while taking a relaxed and self-indulgent break.

TERRITORIAL SURVIVAL: NEEDS AND BARRIERS

Need for Status: People want to feel that they have high standing and prestige in society and in their communities. They want to feel special, to feel that they have earned their position and that they are leaders. Status equals respect and admiration from family, friends, colleagues, peers, mentors and neighbors. People like to "show off" their standing in society by having the latest, greatest or most expensive products, including cars, watches, handbags, jewelry and homes. The Need for Status is the primary reason that people buy luxury car brands such as Cadillac, Lincoln and Lexus. The Need for Status arises in a wide range of product categories. In a project for a company that makes lawn products, we learned that people who fertilize and seed their own grass feel that their lawns reflect their standing in the neighborhood. People take great pride in grooming their yards themselves. In order to maintain their status as upstanding, respectful members of the community, they choose well known brands of lawn products even when they read that less expensive store brands have the same formulas. Why? There is just too much at risk for them to try a store brand that might fail and burn their grass, thereby causing them to lose status in the eyes of their neighbors.

Need for Power: People want to feel strong and dominant over other people and over certain situations. Some people are known as "power hungry"—willing to do just about anything to establish authority and "push their weight around." With power comes control and vice versa, depending on the situation. However, the Need for Power is more about domination over something or someone than it is about control. We saw a clear example of this need while working for a company that makes fire engines. Firefighters draw power from the fire engine because it gives them the feeling that they have super human abilities and it allows them to deny their vulnerability and feel like superheroes. The ideal fire engine brand reassures firefighters that they will be able to operate the apparatus confidently and competently, and will therefore be empowered to do things that ordinary humans cannot do.

Fear of Loss of Family: People feel strongly that their families give meaning to their lives. Without their families, many feel adrift and lonely, because they miss being with people who share their past and their values. An example of this barrier emerges in the automotive market where cramped quarters on long trips and even during every day carpooling makes children fussy and irritable, thereby stressing the driver and interfering with family bonding. People buy expensive mini-vans to insure that all of the children as well as the adults have their own personal space in the vehicle. Consumers buy larger vehicles than the practical needs of their families dictate. Chrysler Corporation's ingenious 2008 upscale mini-van certainly addresses the Fear of Loss of Family by introducing features that make it look and feel a bit like a motor home, such as removable tables, swivel chairs and multiple screens for DVDs. The area behind the front seat becomes a veritable living room, which helps to preserve the integrity of the family.

SEXUAL SURVIVAL: NEEDS AND BARRIERS

Need for Gender Identity: Everyone wants to feel either masculine or feminine. The Need for Gender Identity is not about sexuality per se, although it does include sexuality. It is much broader. When working for an automobile manufacturer on a compact pick-up truck project, respondents told us that their trucks allow them to do manly things—things that men do for themselves, for their families and for their friends and neighbors. Their trucks allow them to do things like move furniture, haul hunting equipment or tools and pull boats—all activities that they view as being masculine. Owning trucks allows them to express their masculine identities and makes them feel like strong and effective men. When a young boy or teenager becomes emotionally attached to trucks and the benefits that they deliver, he will almost always own a truck of some type for the rest of his life.

Need for Intimacy: People want to feel close to others. Intimacy requires very close contact, familiarity and association with other people. Intimacy is a two-way street—it is the willingness to know others and to be known by others. In a project we conducted for a national jewelry retailer, we learned that women want their men to choose jewelry for them without overtly telling them what to buy. They drop hints to their significant others by casually commenting on a friend's piece of jewelry or strategically placing a magazine ad in a visible place or enlisting their young daughters in a "plot" to give daddy hints about what they would love to be able to wear. These women do not want to tell their men directly to purchase a specific piece of jewelry. They want their men to know them well enough to pick the right items without being told what to do. When their men select the right item of jewelry, the women feel that their men know them intimately and feel reassured that they are soulfully connected.

Fear of Boredom/Stagnation: People want to be engaged in activities that stimulate their minds and their emotions. When people are not engaged in activities that nurture their personalities, they begin to feel they are stagnating, which is a kind of death of the core self. When people are bored, they lack stimulation. The diet plan industry provides an excellent example of this barrier. In a project for a diet plan, respondents say dieting can be very tedious, so they reject the rigid and structured plans to avoid feeling deprived of stimulation and variety. The diet and meal programs that have survived in this industry have stayed in business by offering new, varied, tasty products that allow their customers to make nearly as many selections as if they were not on a diet at all.

PHYSICAL SURVIVAL: NEEDS AND BARRIERS

Need for Self-indulgence: From time to time people want to be able to engage in activities purely for themselves, activities that provide them with personal delight and physical pleasure. In a project for a specialty bath products company, we found that women set aside time for themselves away from their families and their children by taking a bath with candles and oils and fragrant soaps. It is indulgent, relaxing and refreshing to take time and space just for themselves, even if it is only for ten or fifteen minutes. By purchasing specialty bath products, these women transform bathing from a utilitarian task into a luxurious, highly personal experience.

Need for Security: People want to feel assured and confident that they can protect themselves and their loved ones from physical and emotional harm. They want to shield themselves from factors in life that cause anxiety and doubt. For example, when people buy life insurance, they are not just buying financial security for others; they are actually buying emotional security for themselves. They are able to alleviate their own anxiety, because they have acquired emotional security for themselves by purchasing emotional and physical security for their families.

Fear of Contamination: People often find that they are afraid that something in a product or service could poison them either physically or mentally. In a project for a distillery, we found that respondents were afraid that the plastic in the jugs that contained the whiskey could slough off into the drink and be toxic for them, causing physical illness and even brain damage. In projects for pharmaceutical companies, it is common for respondents to mention that they fear being harmed by medications that are new to them. In fact, the fear of contamination is one of the major causes of patient non-compliance that drives physicians to extreme states of frustration, because it is a struggle to find ways to reassure their patients about the safety of some drugs, especially new ones.

We have discussed examples of the emotional needs and barriers that comprise the Taxonomy solely in terms of consumer behavior and consumer decisions. However, these needs and barriers explain all of human behavior. They apply to the decisions that people make in their everyday lives, including decisions such as:

- Moving
- Quitting a job
- Going to school
- Choosing which school to go to
- Having a pet
- Having children
- Going to church
- Dating

• Getting married

These everyday decisions are driven by emotional needs and barriers.

When we interview people on a project, we find that the vast majority is motivated to buy the product or brand by the same needs and barriers. Therefore, we see that deep down, on an emotional level, people are more alike than they are different. Armed with our understanding of how people's minds work and our Taxonomy of Emotional Needs and Barriers, we are able to provide accurate insights into why consumers buy and how to motivate them to buy more.

With this taxonomy, The Right Brain Approach is the most comprehensive model of consumer motivation available. It provides business decision makers with the only framework for explaining human behavior.

CHAPTER TWELVE

>━▷━◦━◁━◦

Right Brain Research Has Universal Validity

"There is '…a cultural complex independent of national
and even of racial boundaries, and of remarkable similarity
throughout the world…'"

— ANANDA K. COOMARASWAMY AS CITED

BY JOSEPH CAMPBELL

The emotional needs and barriers in our taxonomy are universal, at least in developed countries. They are present among all peoples in the Western Hemisphere and in the Eastern Hemisphere. They are present regardless of gender, race, nationality or religion.

We cannot say for sure if these needs are innate, but we do know that they arise wherever and whenever man begins to acquire property and asserts his right to hold it and protect it. When man becomes a consumer, the needs and barriers begin to influence his behavior. In fact, the emotional needs and barriers explain why man becomes a consumer and a landholder in the first place!

Even primitive man demonstrated some of the needs in all four survival areas described in the previous chapter. Until the time of consumerism, man was exclusively focused on meeting his physical survival needs. When he stopped wandering, settled down on "his" land and started to plant things, he began meeting needs for territorial survival. We can see how man expressed his need for sexual survival through the proliferation of tribes and communities. Man demonstrated spiritual survival needs by engaging in sun worship and in ritualistic ceremonies that related to the cycles of nature. The Stonehenge monument in England, the Pyramids in Egypt and in the Americas and Newgrange in Ireland are all wonderful examples of how man focused his time and energy on the cycles of nature. So, we can say that early man began to demonstrate spiritual survival needs at least 6,000 years ago and probably as long as 10,000 years ago. There is a wonderful new book titled *Inside the Neolithic Mind* by David Lewis-Williams and David Pearce that documents these basic facts.

From the time that early man began to settle into caves and farms, becoming a gatherer as well as a hunter, common themes across cultures and across continents emerged. East and West share similarities in terms of man's myths, sacrifices, sun worshipping and burial practices. For example, mummies have been found in Egypt, on the Western edge of the Andes and in Urumuchi, China. Joseph Campbell, an American mythology professor best known for his work in comparative mythology and comparative religion, argues persuasively that myths about life, death and sacrifice insinuated themselves into the human psyche to such an extent that they came to be the fundamental organizing principle of human experience. In short, when it comes to how the mind works and what is in it, the ideas man holds and what drives him, we are far more alike no matter where we live than we realize.

In the present day, we find that consumer needs in the four survival areas motivate a vast array of buying behavior that accounts for more than half of the economic activity in the civilized world. We see the universality of the needs and barriers most directly in our research projects. Since 1972 we have interviewed thousands of people who were born in another country, speak a language other than English as their native language and did not come to America until they reached the age of 18. The number of different countries represented by these respondents easily exceeds 30 and spans all of the continents of the globe. Although raised in different cultures and speaking different languages, none of these people have ever communicated a different set of emotional needs driving their behavior.

- For example, a Thai couple in their middle twenties with two children buys a mini-van to fulfill the same emotional needs as a young couple raised on the farms of Nebraska who also buys a mini-van. Both couples want to nurture their children, while at the same time providing an escape experience for everyone, including themselves. The physical space, the seating arrangements, the DVD player, the armrests and the cup holders all contribute to the owners feeling that they are able to control the environment inside the van, giving everyone his own space, while at the same time, keeping the family together.

- A young New York cab driver born and raised in Palestine saves his money and buys upscale stereo components, seeking the same psychological experience as a grad student from MIT. Both are seeking escape, but it is different from the kind of escape that the families with the mini-vans seek. It is much more personal and becomes a solipsistic experience for both of them.

- A married woman in her forties shopping for fragrance in a Paris department store buys Chanel No. 5 fragrance. She is seeking to fulfill the same needs as a single woman in her late twenties from Shanghai who buys the same brand. Both are motivated by the need for hope and they both find it in the same brand.

Discovering universals in human motivation should not be surprising. How else can we explain the worldwide success of such great brands as Marlboro, Starbucks, Guinness, Levi's and McDonald's? Without consumer needs that are universal, it would be impossible to have global brands.

Do we find that there are some differences across countries and cultures? Are there cross-cultural differences that impact messaging? Certainly!

Despite the differences that may exist, we start with the similarities. We always look for how segments of consumers are alike first, whether they are age cohorts in the USA, ethnic groups or consumers from different countries. We analyze the interviews so that we can uncover the needs and barriers that are common to all of the respondents.

Once we uncover the similarities, then we turn to differences. We always find that the Psychological Dynamics driving consumer decisions and behavior are the same across countries and cultures, but the rank order of the needs and barriers may vary from country to country. Because of the universality of the needs and barriers, it is possible to discover the emotional needs and barriers for a brand by visiting a small number of countries and then conducting quantitative studies to uncover differences in how emotional needs are prioritized in the consumer's mind in each country.

Global brands begin by meeting universal needs. Then, in order to localize effectively, they must make sure that they do not stub their toes on cultural differences. Abbott introduced Kaletra, the HIV/AIDS cocktail drug, in Mediterranean countries, but the visual imagery in the advertising that had worked so effectively in the States evoked a much different emotional reaction there. Instead of seeing strong and competent men, the Italians and Spanish in the target audience were offended by the men flaunting their sexuality. The explanation for the differences in emotional reactions to this ad can be found in cultural differences rather than emotional factors. The emotional needs were the same and the messaging needed to be the same, but the execution of the message had to be different in order to take subtle cultural differences into account.

When we first conducted Right Brain Interviews with non-English speaking respondents, we made a delightful discovery: translation is easier than we had ever imagined! The reason is that a Right Brain Interview does not unfold like a conversation. The pace and rhythm of Right Brain Interviews is much different than everyday speech patterns. Analysts use their voices, adjusting both the volume and modulation, to control the interview. The analysts speak softly and slowly, modeling the process for the respondent. Therefore, respondents begin to slow down and speak more softly. There are frequent pauses and moments of silence, all of which facilitates the translation process more than any other methodology could.

Best of all, translation does not have to wait until later. We conduct a modified form of simultaneous translation. Clients can observe and follow the interviews, because everything that respondents and analysts say is translated as the interview unfolds.

If you have ever tried to listen to a focus group, a triad or a one-on-one interview while it is being translated, you will appreciate the convenience and benefit of The Right Brain Approach for interviewing people in their native languages. The pace of the interview with other qualitative methods is much faster and, as a result, content can be lost in translation in real time. In focus groups, there are always times when more than one person is talking and when the pace accelerates, both of which cause some of the most crucial information to be lost.

The emotional needs and barriers in our Taxonomy that explain consumer motivation are the same needs and barriers that underlie all of human behavior. They drive people to do what they do in all aspects of their lives from raising a family to going to school, from building a career to pursuing leisure, from traveling to learning, teaching, loving and just plain living. We gain insight into consumer behavior by looking at the same emotional engine that drives all of human behavior—the ultimate proof that Right Brain Research is universal.

CHAPTER THIRTEEN

Qualitative vs. Quantitative

Which comes first, the chicken or the egg?
— UNKNOWN

When looking to find answers about their customers, marketing executives are often unsure about how and where to start, what type of research to conduct and what to do with the information that the research reveals.

Market research is not just a series of ad hoc projects. Good market research for a brand or product begins with a plan to conduct a sequence of research projects. The most effective way to do that is for qualitative and quantitative research to work in tandem so that the questions raised by quantitative research point toward specific qualitative projects. In turn, the surprises and discoveries from qualitative research inform and inspire further quantitative research. One project gives birth to the next project and so on. The process is a circular one which leads to the question, "Which comes first: quantitative or qualitative?"

When starting with a quantitative survey such as attitude and usage or segmentation, marketers sit down and come up with a list of objectives for the research, and through this process, they come up with questions that they want to answer. They are looking for brand attitudes and usage. They are looking for brand awareness. They are looking for buying predispositions and brand preferences. They are assessing where their brand stands in relationship to other brands. The problem with this commonly used approach is that it imposes a single framework on all brands and products.

When following this single framework, the researchers are unaware of what kind of brand language to use, what is important to people about the product they are researching and what key words and phrases are important to consumers (i.e., the lexicon). And, most importantly, they are not aware of the emotional needs and barriers that are driving behavior in the category. In a nutshell, how do the researchers know what questions to ask? In many cases they do not know. Instead, they simply guess, relying on their own perspectives and their own framework. This guesswork can threaten the future of the brand.

Sometimes people start with focus groups to "get at" how consumers talk about the products and the brands in the category. But, group dynamics tend to take over and too often groups lead to a collection of rationalizations rather than any in-depth understanding of consumer motivation.

For all of these reasons and more, it is far better to start with qualitative rather than quantitative research. In-depth qualitative research provides information about how the consumer feels about the product, talks about the product, uses the product and makes decisions about the product. It also uncovers the attributes of the product and the brand that consumers feel are important. In-depth qualitative research delivers the following:

- What is important to consumers
- What questions to ask
- How to ask them
- And, what words to use

This information provides inspiration and direction for writing an effective questionnaire and developing a powerful research design. The Sterling story illustrates these points.

In 1994, Sterling, the second largest retail jewelry company in the country, established a full-fledged market research department. One of the first objectives for Sterling's market research department was to identify segments of consumers in the jewelry marketplace. However, as they embarked on the process of conducting this quantitative work, they realized that they did not have enough information about their customers to write the segmentation questionnaire. They decided that they needed basic information about the jewelry category and what motivates consumers in this category before rushing headlong into quantitative work.

Sterling developed a multi-stage plan that started off with Right Brain Research that provided them with an understanding of what motivates the jewelry consumer. This in-depth emotional understanding of their jewelry customers inspired and drove the design of subsequent quantitative projects. It helped them determine what kinds of questions to ask and it helped them craft the language to use in their questionnaires.

Sterling's Market Research Department was able to add value to their business by turning their request for a research project into a plan for building Sterling's business. The lesson is clear: when in doubt, the right path is usually to conduct qualitative research first because it will drive the design of all subsequent quantitative research.

When the marketers start off on the right foot with qualitative, they will find themselves moving down a path where the quantitative research will return the favor. Quantitative projects designed with the right questions and the right language asked in the right way lead to results that beg for further understanding and explanation. In other words, another round of qualitative naturally flows from this process.

Sterling's flagship brand is Kay° Jewelers — the second largest mall-based jewelry chain after Zales. With the right foundation established by Right Brain Research, Sterling moved to segmentation and other more advanced quantitative research techniques. That was in 1995. Today, Kay® is a dynamic brand in the marketplace and has surpassed Zales in profitability if not in size. According to a recent article in *The Wall Street Journal*, Zales is way behind.

Sterling's choice to use qualitative findings as a launch pad for their overall research strategy is just the beginning of their success story. Because mall-based stores such as Kay® are constrained by space and many other factors controlled by the shopping mall, Sterling's managers were also working on new store designs. They were able to incorporate the findings from the qualitative research into the design of an entirely new store concept.

They named the new store Jared® The Galleria of Jewelry. The research results drove the store design and the architecture of the brand in the following areas:

• Décor

• Lighting

• Store layout

• Furniture

• Employee training, orienting them to focus on the experience of the customer

• Refreshments for customers

• Selection

• Product layout

You can learn about great brands by seeing Jared® in action. So, do yourself a favor! Visit the largest shopping mall in your community. Visit all the mall-based stores. Talk to the salespeople and look at the merchandise. Then go to the nearest Jared® store. You will not find it in the mall. It is a free-standing store. Focus on what makes it different from the mall stores and what makes it different from any other jewelry store you have ever visited. Notice the difference in the décor, the service, the merchandise and, most of all, how the salespeople treat you. It is unique. It is an entirely different experience from visiting a mall-based store, a private jeweler or any other jewelry store.

Jared® is the fastest growing and most popular jewelry chain in the country. It is a great brand! Analyze it and see if you can figure out what makes it so great. They did not succeed through guesswork. They succeeded by following through on a strategic research plan using both qualitative and quantitative research. They found out what people really want when they shop for jewelry, they gave it to them and then they consistently managed the brand over time so that it has not lost its appeal. They understand that a great brand is so much more than the product. They realize that the product is necessary, but more importantly that the product is not sufficient to guarantee their success.

PART III
WHAT HAPPENS WHEN YOU FOLLOW THE RIGHT BRAIN WAY?

CHAPTER FOURTEEN

>─◄◆►─○─◄◆►─◄

Positioning Silver Dollar City

"Without a good sense of what your customer believes,
knows and dreams about your business,
you don't stand much of a chance of walking
through the door that will match who you are to those same
beliefs, knowledge or dreams."
—PETER HERSCHEND, CO-FOUNDER & CO-OWNER,
HERSCHEND FAMILY ENTERTAINMENT

In 1976 I met Pete HERSCHEND, Vice President of Marketing and co-owner of Silver Dollar City. The City is a theme park in the southern Ozarks and the anchor attraction in a then little known town of 5,000 people, a town named Branson.

Pete hired us to serve as his consultants for developing a long-range strategic plan to grow the size of the City. He asked about the experience people have when they visit the City. He wanted to know WHY people visit the City. He had the answers to a lot of other questions, including:

- Who comes to Silver Dollar City?

- Where do they come from?

- How many came?

- When do they come?
- How do they get there?
- Who told them to come?
- How much do they spend?
- What do they buy when they arrive?
- What part of the City do they like best?
- What part do they like least?

But, he did not know why they come and why they come back, why they spend so much money, why they like the things that they like and why they dislike the things that they dislike.

He figured if he could answer these questions, he could plan the direction for the development of the City. He would know what kind of a place it should try to be. We tapped into the emotional mind of the visitors to find out why they come. What we found is that the visitors to the City, especially the ones who buy season passes and return again and again, are looking for a very specific kind of experience. It is almost as though they want to get on a time machine and go backwards in time, back to a time when things are simple, when life is easier. They really want to lose themselves—lose themselves in space and time. They enter a different zone, where their anxieties go away and they just feel better. They are fulfilling a very specific emotional need, the Need to Escape.

They lose track of time and become part of the life of the City. They eat the food, sing the songs, socialize, play and even work like the people in the City. We call this an escape experience because it is as though they are in a different time and place altogether, allowing them to escape their worries and problems, and most importantly to escape their internal conflicts.

We found that management had built in a lot of experiences that help the visitors escape. For example, the City has rides, which are lots of fun, but they are not thrill rides like one finds at Six Flags. One ride, which is an "experience" called "Fire in the Hole," is an underground ride into an 1880s village that is on fire. It is a bit scary and a bit threatening, but very enjoyable too because by the time the ride gets to the fire in the hole, the people on the ride feel like they are part of the village. The village's survival is threatened, so their survival is threatened too and everyone on the ride and everyone in the village triumphs in the end. The people on the ride feel like they helped put the fire out and helped to save the village. This involvement in the experience makes them slip even further into the feeling of escaping to a different time and place.

The key is how Silver Dollar City encourages its visitors to escape. It turns out that many little things work together to support, encourage and maintain the visitor's overall escape experience. For example, visitors to the park encounter an undertaker with a stovepipe hat who measures people for caskets. Then, they witness an impassioned soapbox speaker who bursts into the saloon, giving a fiery speech about temperance. These details contribute to the palpable feeling of being suspended in another time and another place and it is as though people are transported back in time to that place!

Clearly the management team at the City was doing a great job, but they had not ever articulated the nature of the visitor's experience. They were making decisions based on intuition without fully realizing why the things that were working worked so well. The challenge for the City was to grow without drifting away from the core of the visitor's experience. Armed with this new insight and understanding, Silver Dollar City had defined its identity for the first time. In marketing terms, it had discovered its position in the mind of the consumer. After struggling for nearly a year to write a coherent positioning statement, it was now a relatively straightforward matter to put it on paper in a way that was compelling and suggested the direction for future development at the City.

The spirit captured by the positioning statement drove product development, communication strategy, new attractions, employee training and financial investments for the next generation.

The results speak for themselves:

- During the gas crisis in the late 1970s, Silver Dollar City was the only destination park in the country that showed an increase in attendance.
- The City became the anchor for the explosive growth of Branson as a tourist destination.
- The number of visitors increased six fold from 1975 to 2000.
- Silver Dollar City was named the top theme park in the world, 1998-1999.
- The success of the City provided a platform for the holding company to develop many successful and profitable new ventures.

Silver Dollar City already had a strong position in the consumer's mind. The City's leaders knew that it had a strong position, but they did not know quite what that position was. They also knew that in order to continue to succeed and grow they needed to develop their business in the right direction.

By uncovering the emotional needs that Silver Dollar City fulfills for its visitors and positioning itself as a theme park that offers an escape experience, the City has been able to achieve phenomenal growth and success.

CHAPTER FIFTEEN

>-I-◆>-O-◆-I-<

The Saturn Story

"The reason Saturn succeeds is not because they make a
better car than say, Honda, but because they over deliver on
their brand promise. It's not the car, it's the car company."
— SCOTT DEMING, "BRILLIANT BRANDERS: 5 COMPANIES
THAT KNOW THE IMPORTANCE OF THE CUSTOMER
EXPERIENCE"

By 1980 General Motors had given up competing with the Japanese
big three: Toyota, Honda and Datsun. GM executives realized that
they had lost the ball game, at least at the low end of the market.
Their products cost more and did not hold up. Yes, it is true. Back
then, Japanese imports were cheaper than domestics! In fact, Detroit
had purposely built small cars to be inferior, on the arrogant assump-
tion that they could teach the American public that small cars are no
good! Needless to say, this folly made it even easier for the Japanese
to succeed.

Ironically, Roger Smith, the Chairman at GM at the time, turned
to the "enemy" and signed a joint venture deal with Toyota, agree-
ing to build cars together. Soon the joint venture's plant in Northern
California was turning Toyota Corollas out one door of the factory
and Geo (Chevrolet) Prisms out the other. It was the same platform,

the same car, two assembly lines and two different badges. Smith's motivation for the joint venture was to learn manufacturing methods from the Japanese, but it was an interim survival strategy in his mind—nothing more.

Meanwhile, Smith turned to the longer-range challenge of how to build good entry-level cars that the American public would buy. Much like the IBM executives who had decided their organization could not produce a desktop computer, Smith concluded that the GM bureaucracy could not turn the tide that was running in Japan's favor. So, he gave his blessing to the Group of 99 at GM, a spontaneous formation of 99 UAW workers and middle managers who came together to talk about how to improve the company and design better cars. Saturn was born and soon it became a separate corporation within the General Motors family.

Smith's grand strategy at this point centered on working around GM's bureaucracy, widespread executive denial and fear of what might happen if major changes were made. So a separate company was the first component of his plan.

To build a successful car company Smith would need several more "parts," however. The fanatically committed Group of 99, of which very little is known even today, provided a second component. A third came from a new manufacturing process imported from Japan. Saturn set out to build a new car from scratch, without owing allegiance to any GM shelf parts or pet suppliers. In fact, Saturn took inspiration from the Japanese and designed the car for manufacturability. Ironically this revolutionary idea would later put some major constraints on the consumer friendliness of the eventual product, because the basic structure of the vehicle (the "envelope" as it is called in the business) was created before consumer input was obtained!

With these components in place, Saturn then asked us to bring our methodology to bear on the question: "What would it take to convince import owners to switch back to a domestic brand, a new one at that?" When we interviewed those import owners, here is what we found. We discovered that people who had switched from domestic brands to import brands did it because of a culmination of bad experiences with American cars. People at the entry level in the marketplace felt that they could not afford to risk their limited economic resources on a car that might break down. Also, they felt that their physical survival would be threatened if they bought another domestic brand. These people took a huge leap and crossed over the Rubicon into foreign territory, leaving the domestic territory behind forever.

Why was this switch such an irreversible step in the mind of consumers? They found almost as many problems with the foreign brands as they had with the domestic brands, yet they had forsaken their country and their patriotism to get there. They had to rationalize and justify their decision by minimizing the problems with the foreign brands and explaining them away. These dynamics were so profound, pervasive and deeply rooted within the consumers' minds that it was going to take a completely different approach to win them back. Good product design and bulletproof reliability would not be enough to guarantee success. In order to succeed, Saturn was going to have to take this game to a new ball field and make some new rules. They were going to have to deliver a completely new shopping and buying experience.

We analyzed all aspects of the car business: shopping, the sales experience, the service experience, warranties, recalls and trade-ins. The answer came back: people were terribly frustrated, intimidated, upset, conflicted and angry over the experience of shopping for a new car. The consumer viewed car dealers as crooks. Consumers had always hated buying cars. It was a painful, anxiety-ridden process involving intimidating salespeople treating customers as fools or idiots. The older, experienced buyer sometimes became inured to the process. A few even learned to make it into a game. But, to the first time/entry-level buyer, a trip to an automobile showroom in the mid 1980s was a horror to be avoided at nearly any cost. Consumers were so turned off that they avoided it as long as possible, whether they were interested in a domestic or an import brand. Although all this is now common knowledge, back then automotive executives had no idea how much damage their companies had done in the minds of consumers. Even today the industry is still largely trapped by ignorance and quite mysteriously seems helpless to change it, because it is part of the business paradigm that prevails in the automotive world. It is still the way that most cars are sold in America.

In the meantime, Saturn got a fresh start and built its own paradigm. The implication was clear; Saturn should change the emotional experience people have when they shop for cars. In fact, the research pointed toward this strategy as an imperative. It was clear that a new domestic company could never compete against Toyota and the others on quality alone. The imports already owned this position in people's heads. Instead, Saturn became the company consumers could trust. It became a company made up of people who treat you with respect, without hassle or intimidation strategies. Saturn turned a disgusting experience into a delightful one and thereby won in the marketplace.

The strategy pointed toward many new and unique approaches in the business. It created a new paradigm that included the following elements:

- **Carefully selected dealers who would commit to the Saturn philosophy:** GM did not allow any of their dealers to add Saturn to their portfolios of brands unless they had very high dealer satisfaction scores.

- **The market area approach:** a retail outlet would be called "Saturn of Minneapolis" instead of "Joe's Saturn." This approach emphasizes the continuity of the brand and also avoids dealers in large markets competing with one another over price.

- **An emphasis on the shopping and buying experience, rather**

than on the product: Initially, the advertising did not even show the product, a first in automotive history. Later, the product showed up, but only as a back drop to the main focus, which was the customer and his or her experience in the store. For example, in an early commercial Susie is taking possession of the keys to her first car and all the Saturn associates form a circle around her, clap and help her celebrate the beginning of a new relationship.

• **Simple, published, no-haggle pricing:** In 1985 and even today, a shopper will find it impossible in many dealerships to find out the price of the car he is interested in. In contradistinction, Saturn adopted a single non-negotiable published price for each of its cars. The automotive writers and "experts" told the Saturn executives and The Right Brain People that this policy would never work and that as soon as there was a downturn in the market, the retailer would cut the prices and if he did not, the customer would demand it! That was 1990 and to this day the new policy we recommended holds! Why? Because it is in line with the emotional needs of the Saturn shoppers.

• **No pressure from salespeople:** The people in the store are associates, not salespeople.

• **Associates are paid by salary instead of commission:** Because they are not paid by commission, they can be equally helpful and pleasant to all shoppers regardless of which Associate is working with the customer. Try to find a salesperson in a Chevrolet dealership who will give you the time of day if you are not his customer (or his mark!) and you will immediately appreciate the powerful advantage that the Saturn brand has over the competition at the entry level.

• **Design of the store to minimize the intimidation factor:** The Saturn store debuted with warm carpeting instead of a cold terrazzo floor, lower ceilings instead of high ceilings that feel intimidating, friendly and helpful associates instead of blustering salesmen and a homey feel instead of a cold, institutional environment. The architects and designers of the Saturn store hit a grand slam home run in creating spaces that are approachable and reassuring for fearful customers.

- **Large window from the showroom into the service bays:** Ironically, these windows were inspired by the one-way windows from the observation room into the interview room in the field service where we conducted interviews that led to these recommendations. In the dealership, the windows allow the prospective customer to imagine that he will be able to see his car worked on by friendly people in a clean, organized shop. This design element communicates that the service department and the shop is an integral part of the overall operation rather than a place that the customer is sent by a nasty manager who washes his hands of the cars that are not working as they are supposed to!

Here is the bottom line: the Saturn plant in Spring Hill, Tennessee, ran at above capacity for the first four years. Saturn sold all the cars the company could make up until around 1995. Since then the factories have run at near capacity virtually all of the time. Saturn has been able to extend the emotional benefit delivered by its brand to events such as the Saturn Homecoming in 1995, when 40,000 Saturn owners and their families came from all over the country to have a picnic and see where their cars were made. Saturn's overwhelming success is now legendary.

Saturn became the cornerstone of GM's success in recapturing competitiveness in the entry-level market. The much-envied J.D. Powers award for #1 in overall dealer satisfaction became Saturn's exclusive property. This accomplishment is not surprising since Saturn built the company on changing the emotional experience of shopping for cars from a misery to a delight. Saturn flirted with the top spot in overall satisfaction, usually coming in a close third behind Lexus and Infiniti—an amazing accomplishment for a car that costs a fraction of these luxury models.

The skeptics inside of GM and throughout the automotive world said it could not be done. But it has been done, and it has been done better than anyone dreamed, because Saturn took The Right Brain Approach and broke new ground by making a new paradigm.

These insights into consumer motivation allowed Saturn to differentiate the brand by redesigning the shopping and the sales experience. Of course the Saturn approach takes the spotlight off the product, which is heresy in the automotive business. The heresy worked. The success story is history.

CHAPTER SIXTEEN

>─◦─<─◦─<

Into the Wild Blue Yonder...
the FAA and STARS

"Right Brain Research has been uniquely and powerfully
effective, because it uncovers the motivation that is the
antecedent to purchase."

—TOM WITTENSCHLAEGER, CHAIRMAN AND CEO,

RAPTOR NETWORKS TECHNOLOGY, INC.

Since 1972 we have worked on many different projects in many categories. It would be very difficult to say which project was the most intriguing. One of the candidates surely would have to be our work at the Hughes Aircraft Company, a Howard Hughes legacy considered a national scientific treasure.

I first met Tom Wittenschlaeger, who wrote the Foreword to this book, in 1993, when he was the Director of Corporate Market Research at Hughes. He was so fascinated by The Right Brain Approach that he traveled to Memphis solely to fully grasp the methodology and to observe a daylong demonstration. Soon I was in Los Angeles at the Hughes corporate headquarters conducting the first in a series of Right Brain Interviews on how the government would go about selecting which companies would win major tasks on the Strategic Defense Initiative (SDI) project, famously referred to as "Star Wars."

After the initial project, Tom came back to us and asked us to analyze a business problem at Hughes. At that time the company was a major government contractor and proudly possessed one of the largest collections of brilliant scientists in the world. Their talent pool of project people holding PhDs and Master's Degrees exceeded 35,000. Hughes Aircraft competed with Bell Labs for the top new talent from each year's graduating class at Caltech and MIT. Hughes offered a classic "Right Brain" advantage to these young, hormonally charged geniuses: take a job with Bell Labs in dreary Holmdel, New Jersey or accept a position at the glass-enshrouded Hughes Research Labs overlooking the pristine beaches of Malibu, California. This "difficult choice" translated into a compelling technology advantage that Hughes Aircraft enjoyed for decades.

Hughes had pioneered the satellite business and had also revolutionized warfare with innovations in sensors, weaponry, displays and systems. From mortar locating radars to night vision systems to torpedoes, Hughes technologies were front row center in winning every major conflict from the Cold War to the Gulf War. Hughes Aircraft was also the #1 worldwide provider of Air Traffic Control Systems and Displays. They had designed, built and delivered entire ATC systems for countries such as Canada.

The real puzzle was that The Federal Aviation Administration (FAA) in the United States, the largest single customer of air traffic control products worldwide, had never selected Hughes. While Hughes had hundreds of contracts with US government entities from the Department of Defense to NASA at that time, they had nary a one with the FAA! Hughes maintained a marketing office in Roslyn, Virginia across the Potomac River from Washington, DC in order to penetrate the vast FAA bureaucracy. But, they had had absolutely no luck, nor did they sense that they were making any progress. Time and again Hughes submitted bids on major RFPs, but somehow never managed to be selected. Each time the reason was different. It made no rational sense to Hughes executives, and they wanted to know why it was happening and what to do about it.

The situation represented a major challenge for Hughes and for us. However, if we could crack the nut, the rewards could be huge. As we reviewed the situation in detail, several unique features of the challenge began to emerge:

- Instead of analyzing a market with many prospects, we were going to have to analyze a single prospect, the FAA.

- We did not have the advantage of interviewing anyone at the FAA who had selected Hughes as a contractor or had even worked with them. This feature of the assignment made the challenge very difficult.

- We were going to have to interview government bureaucrats in their places of business. This requirement was a huge burden. Instead of us being in control, the respondents were going to be in control. If a phone call came in, they would interrupt the interview. They felt like they were in charge in their offices where they were used to doing things their way, rather than being in a field service setting, an unfamiliar environment where they would have felt less in control.

- Because we had to interview FAA respondents in their offices during work hours, we could not pay them the usual incentives. So, instead of working for us for 90 minutes and having to do what we wanted them to do for that time, as is normally the case, they did not really have to do anything we wanted them to do. This fact was underscored when one of our senior analysts interviewed his first FAA employee. The respondent had ordered pizza to eat during the interview. Not only did he refuse to close his eyes and wear the visualization mask, but he also ate pizza during the entire interview. And, he did not even share a slice!

- There were not enough FAA employees to meet our requirements, so we interviewed proxies. In this case, the proxies were consultants. They were former FAA employees who had participated in contract decisions while in the employ of the government, and had transitioned to the private sector by the time that the Right Brain Interviews were conducted. The advantage of using proxies is that they are likely to be much more open than current employees; the disadvantage is that they could be out of touch with recent changes and current developments. All in all, however, the proxies turned out to be wonderful substitutes in this and many other projects for Hughes. We always recruited recent retirees so we could be certain that the respondents we interviewed would still be in touch with the situation — in this case, the situation at the FAA. Another reason why proxies worked so well for us is that we asked our respondents to go back in their minds' eyes to a time that stood out for them when they were making a difficult decision. When respondents do this, they are actually reliving past experiences. So, in this situation, the fact that they were not current employees made no difference in the interview process. We were able to use the same interview guide for the proxies that we used with the FAA employees.

We faced significant challenges in this project, but because our methodology is so robust and malleable, we were able to deal with the challenges inherent in the situation. What did we discover?

The Finding

Surprisingly, the FAA was well aware of the brilliance, education, creativity and track record of the Hughes team. So, from a rational or left brain perspective, they admitted openly that Hughes was superior to its competitors on this basis. However, this advantage was clearly not sufficient for Hughes to be selected.

The primary insight was that the FAA executives saw technologists from Hughes as being arrogant, and rejected them for this reason. From an emotional or right brain perspective, the FAA was simply unwilling to endure the emotional pain that they imagined they would have to experience while working with an obnoxious but brilliant Hughes team for a span of years. They were unwilling to put up with Hughes' arrogance and so awarded contracts to technically inferior providers.

The Expectations

We discovered that the FAA executives held highly irrational expectations of their contractors, compared to what we had seen elsewhere. FAA executives were almost all career lawyers and consultants rather than engineers. They expected their industry partners to work for nothing for years, carrying the FAA's water up to Capitol Hill and helping sell the FAA program proposals to Congress. Additionally, they expected all of their critical contractors to be accessible to them — which meant relocating major operations to within 25 miles of FAA headquarters in Washington. Finally, the FAA expected its potential contractors to socialize themselves to the agency, investing personal, technical and programmatic support for free in the hope of gaining sufficient trust to be awarded an initial contract. Doing so generally required hundreds of man-years and tens of millions of dollars invested on the contractor's part before the first contract was ever signed! In the corporate world, expectations like this from a supplier relationship would never be accommodated, but in the strange world of government contracting, such expectations of contractors are par for the course — at least they were in those years. A picture emerged clarifying the underlying causality for endemic overspending and programmatic underperformance in our nation's Capitol.

Not surprisingly, this discovery was a tough pill to swallow for Hughes. They were aware of these perceptions and expectations on a much smaller scale. Everyone who does business with the government knows about it, but the scope, intensity and the extent of the correction that Hughes executives would have to make in order to succeed was a revelation to them.

What Hughes Had to Do!

The mandate for Hughes was simple:

1. Change the perceptions held by the FAA about the arrogance and attitude at Hughes. Perhaps even change out the most arrogant people themselves.

2. Move the operational headquarters of the ATC business to within 25 miles of FAA headquarters in Washington, DC.

3. Become a free "support asset" to the FAA, working and investing to earn sufficient trust to "join the family."

It worked! Within eight months, Hughes had won a $200,000,000 support contract by institutionalizing the first recommendation above. Twelve months thereafter the Hughes-Raytheon team defeated Lockheed Martin, a much larger and far better financed competitor, and won the lucrative FAA STARS (Standard Terminal Automation Replacement System) development project.

"What is a development contract?" you might ask. Simply put, it is a chance to design, build, deliver, install and launch a breakthrough new system that will remain in place for decades. Once a company does so, the residual expertise within the organization generates collateral business value in adjacent businesses such as international ATC, Air Defense and innumerable others. Hughes went to work, investing millions in testing engineering prototypes, software and communications systems and postulated what the architecture of the system should look like. When the FAA issued its RFP, many global companies that were technically qualified to do the work positioned themselves to bid on it. Hughes won a major piece, and in doing so secured a $1.6B contract.

The contract that Hughes won led to the design and build out of an entirely new generation of air traffic control systems. The new system modernized a dangerously aging element of critical infrastructure, providing much greater capacity, flexibility and immediacy of control. The program manages and routes commercial airliners anytime they fly above 24,500 feet in the domestic United States. Basically, it keeps all of our planes up in the air and prevents them from crashing into one another at cruise altitude—something all of us appreciate when we travel!

Tom gives us the lion's share of the credit for the $1.6B worth of business that he won when his team embraced the Right Brain Research findings. He muses that Hughes would never have received its first contract with the FAA had we not shown them the true nature of the problem and how to turn it around. The greatest irony, in his eyes, was that scores of trusted, seasoned insiders, both at Hughes and at Raytheon, had advised their senior management so incorrectly that without the Right Brain Research, neither team would have had a prayer at winning the STARS program. These were absolutely brilliant people who were brilliantly wrong.

Hughes won because their senior managers set "conventional wisdom" aside, saw and admitted to the problem they had created for themselves, ignored their inside "experts" and collectively took an enormous career risk by trying something completely different. Ironically, the string of successes that followed illustrated that the greatest actual risk they had endured was allowing the status quo to persist for so long. We were pleased to have been the catalyst for the Hughes successes.

CHAPTER SEVENTEEN

>----»--◦--«----<

Right Brain Strategy Development

"Alone we can do so little; together we can do so much."
— HELEN KELLER

Brand strategy development in business today often falls short of being the invaluable management and leadership tool that it can be. The first problem is that companies often approach the development of a brand in a purely left brain way. Strategy is based on highlighting rational product attributes rather than the emotional benefits that the consumer experiences. Since the strategy is based on a purely left brain approach, the objectives to support the strategy and the way the objectives are measured are also driven by left brain thinking. The emotional connection between the consumer and the brand is not factored into the strategy and it is not measured as the brand develops.

The second problem is that many companies treat brand strategy as the sole responsibility of the marketing department. Just as finance does not own profitability, because everyone in the company must contribute to it, so also marketing should not hold sole responsibility for brand strategy. We have learned that the companies with the most successful brands hold that everyone in the company has responsibility for supporting a brand's strategy. A brand strategy is all encompassing; it must include the entire company and be incorporated into every part of an organization in order to be successful.

Our process for developing brand strategy ensures a balance between left brain and right brain elements and includes representation from all parts of an organization.

When Abbott introduced Kaletra, it was quickly recognized as the strongest cocktail drug for HIV/AIDS patients. Abbott and its healthcare ad agency had positioned the product based on the significant product attributes of strength and tolerability. Kaletra became the number one drug in the market rather quickly. Then, gradually, it began to lose sales. It dropped to number two and then to number three. Abbott decided to take a step back and look at the brand and consider a repositioning or a re-launch. They were familiar with our work and with our ability to answer "why" questions and we had worked on a significant new product introduction previously for them. They hired us to figure out why the sales of Kaletra had dropped and how to reverse the trend.

We started by conducting Right Brain Interviews with patients and prescribing physicians. The brand team at Abbott wanted us to uncover the emotional underpinnings of what they perceived to be the three main advantages of Kaletra: strength, durability and endurance. During the interviews, we did not discover significant emotional ties to these product attributes, so we ended up taking a much more open ended approach with our probing. We discovered that control was the key emotional benefit that patients were seeking.

When patients experienced a spike in their viral load, they felt out of control of their work lives, their social lives and their sex lives. They felt like they were not themselves any more. They experienced a threat to their self-identities because they felt like they had been knocked out of the game of life. They could not have normal relationships with other people. They wanted to get back in control and recapture the lives they had before they were diagnosed with HIV. In order to achieve this return to their former lives and their former selves, their viral load had to be undetectable. The word undetectable was powerful because it had multiple meanings. On the surface, it meant that the viral load was down to the point where the medical test did not reveal the presence of the virus. On a deeper level, it meant that patients were not even aware of being sick. They did not feel sick. Nor did they feel that their friends and co-workers perceived them as being sick. The emotional benefit for these patients, then, was being in control again and recapturing their self-identities by getting their lives back.

During the interviews with the physicians, we discovered that when Kaletra first came out, they had prescribed it as a first line drug because of its strength. However, after patients had been on Kaletra for awhile and their viral load increased, there was no second line drug for the physicians to prescribe that was stronger than Kaletra. So, physicians began to drop Kaletra as a first line drug because without having a second line option, they felt that they were failing their patients.

We also discovered that these physicians felt very emotionally connected to their patients. Choosing to treat HIV/AIDS patients represented a time commitment for the physicians because these patients required long-term care and frequent office visits. And, in order to build expertise and knowledge, these doctors had to dedicate a significant part of their practices to HIV/AIDS patients. The physicians committed to treating these patients because they sympathized with their plight as outcasts who felt that their lives were slipping away from them. The doctors wanted to make a significant difference in these patients' lives. The relevance of the physicians' emotional connection to the patients was that the messaging strategy to the patients needed to resonate with the physicians as well.

As a result of the Right Brain Interviews with the patients and physicians, we recommended that Abbott stop focusing on strength, endurance and durability which are all left brain product attributes, and instead focus on helping patients gain control of their lives. This strategy addressed the emotional needs of both the patients and the physicians.

Armed with this powerful insight about how patients and physicians connect emotionally to the Kaletra brand, we conducted an off-site work session to develop a Brand Promise. The brand strategy development team included people from a number of different departments at Abbott as well as their advertising agencies. The team worked in groups on several assignments designed to draw out creative and intuitive faculties. These exercises allow the participants to think, create and problem solve in a way that they normally do not do on a daily basis as they juggle the demands of meetings, emails and phone calls. The two best examples of exercises that draw out this creativity are the room exercise and the future story.

In the room exercise, we asked the participants to create a room that encapsulated the essence of the Kaletra brand. The description had to include the furniture, music, colors, paintings and design of the room as well as people in the room and activities that occurred there. This exercise was incredibly powerful because from a process standpoint, the participants did something that they do not ever do. They were taken completely out of their everyday work mentality and were asked to create something out of nothing, purely on the basis of their imagination and their creativity. The constraint was that they had to be able to explain how the room they created tied into the research findings and the brand. This exercise took the team beyond the product attributes into the intangible qualities of the brand and how the brand makes people feel, which is what the brand is all about. The participants had to get beyond the literal characteristics of the product and explore the connotative meaning of the brand. They had to articulate the messages that the brand conveyed, as well as the metaphors and the symbols that it suggested. In this exercise, once people started generating suggestions, the dam broke and ideas started flooding out.

People got very excited about what they were creating. The energy in the room was palpable.

Next, the team worked on the future story. Each participant wrote a story about what the brand will look like, what it will be doing and what it will have accomplished in five years' time. They had to visualize a story about the brand as it would appear in *The Wall Street Journal* or *Fortune*. The story had to include what the brand team did to get there. This exercise was very powerful. It took people out of their rational mindset and inspired them to imagine, invent, create and outline what they could do to make their dreams happen.

In the February 2005 issue of *Pharmaceutical Executive*, Skip Thurnauer wrote an article about Abbott's brand strategy development, which has inspired this chapter. He wrote, "Right Brain Research also took the team to a place it had not explored before: the heart. By better understanding the feelings of patients and physicians, it developed a new brand promise and an effective new advertising campaign that has helped Kaletra maintain its position as the number one protease inhibitor."

HIV/AIDS patients want their lives back again. They want to regain control. They want their disease to be undetectable to the lab, to their friends and to themselves. And their physicians want to help them achieve those goals. Communicating these emotional benefits as opposed to the rational product attributes was the key to repositioning the brand. Soon Kaletra had regained the number one position in the marketplace.

CHAPTER EIGHTEEN

>-+-»-o-«-+-<

The Right Brain Approach
Gets Results

"However beautiful the strategy, you should
occasionally look at the results."

— WINSTON CHURCHILL

The Right Brain People has successfully applied the Right Brain
Methodology to the following business challenges:

- Strategic planning and direction
- Brand strategy
- Product development
- Customer satisfaction
- Human resources
- Service quality
- Advertising impact
- Corporate and brand image

Some key success appear below:

- **Corvette:** In 1988 the future of Corvette was threatened. The
brand was dropping in sales and losing a substantial amount

of money. Despite its icon status in the automotive world and in America, GM executives were seriously considering phasing the Corvette out. A few zealots at the company championed the brand and brought us in to conduct a comprehensive program on the emotional appeal of Corvette. We provided the psychological foundation for the design and introduction of the 1993 model, saving the brand, doubling its sales and transforming it from a losing platform into a brand that delivers a $350M gross profit annually.

• **Elvis Presley Enterprises:** Based on Right Brain Research we developed an emotional profile of Elvis fans who visited Graceland. The visitor's experience was designed and structured around understanding Elvis' unique appeal at the emotional level. We found that Elvis' secret lies in his ability to give people absolution and permission to have sexual feelings! Graceland became the #1 tourist attraction in the state of Tennessee, welcoming over 700,000 visitors annually from all 50 states and over 80 foreign countries. We conducted emotional research on why people visit Elvis' grave and then recommended 33 action steps that saved the estate from bankruptcy, eventually leading to annual revenue of $45M and a sale of most of the assets of the estate for nearly $100M.

• **Maybelline** achieved a 37.5% increase in nationwide market share, surpassing its two competitors, Cover Girl and Revlon, both of which had much larger advertising budgets and better distribution.

• **Zuri Cosmetics** was able to establish an understanding of the consumer mindset to develop a single 30-second commercial, which quadrupled sales in Walgreen's nationwide and catapulted it to the #1 African American cosmetic brand.

- **A major cooking oil brand** increased market share by making several subtle but important changes in their package design, based on consumer perceptions and emotional needs.

- **A boxed juice product** increased sales dramatically by redesigning its packaging as a result of the findings from a Right Brain project.

- **A statewide hospital system's cardiovascular program generated an average** of 1,000 calls and 300 appointments per month, starting from a base of zero. The result increased bed utilization so that the hospital's census increased to 100%.

- **In Arkansas a highly controversial statewide referendum** passed after having been defeated 2 to 1 twice in the past. In effect voters did the impossible. They voted to change the state constitution to permit banks to charge higher interest rates on consumer loans.

- **Working together, Family Research Council and the National Council for Adoption** supported a project to discover the barriers to choosing adoption among women agonizing over unwanted, unplanned pregnancies. The project also included a group of counselors who work with these women. The National Council for Adoption relied heavily on the findings to design the first nationwide program to educate counselors on adoption as a viable alternative for women who feel they cannot raise their children. The program was funded by the Infant Adoption Awareness Act of 2001. We conducted a second project to understand why birthmothers decide to place their children for adoption. The results are published by the National Council for Adoption and Family Research Council in an article titled "BIRTHMOTHER, GOOD MOTHER." In 2008 there will be a national campaign targeted to women with unwanted, unplanned pregnancies, promoting adoption as a viable alternative.

- **Methodist Hospital in Memphis, the 4th largest non-profit hospital system in the world,** reduced nurse turnover in a Critical Care Unit from 65% to 15%.

The Right Brain Approach gives our clients a distinct advantage over the competition — the advantage of understanding what really motivates consumers to buy. With this knowledge, companies can create strategies that fulfill genuine needs, thereby strengthening their positions in the marketplace, intensifying customer loyalty and increasing sales.

CONCLUSION

>-↠-◦-↞-◅

WHERE THERE IS A WILL,
THERE IS A WAY!

The Right Brain Way describes a way of doing business that will inevitably lead to success. You should now have a clear picture of what it takes to build and sustain a successful brand. Successful brand building not only takes time and money and a winning strategy...it also takes "guts."

For Tom Wittenschlaeger, the Hughes Aircraft Company wunderkind, who authored the Foreword to this book, success at Hughes included going against the grain at times. In one instance, which he aptly describes as a "bet-your-career" move, Wittenschlaeger had to fight tradition and override the conventional wisdom of his colleagues, trusting instead the findings revealed through Right Brain Research. You do not make decisions like that haphazardly or without good reason. Certainly Tom did not, nor should you. So why did he do it?

One reason: Tom knew something that none of the Hughes engineers involved in preparing proposals to the FAA knew. He knew that <u>Hughes could absolutely trust the results and recommendations of Right Brain Research</u>!

Tom had made the leap. His mental paradigm regarding marketing research methodologies had shifted, so that he could see and trust what others at the company had not yet discovered. He had found a

143

way to "T-Bone" the competition, by acting on strategic insights about his prospects that could not be accessed by any other means.

As a result, it did not matter what the vast majority of his colleagues thought about The Right Brain Approach verses traditional methods. His job was not to perpetuate the status quo. His job was to win business for Hughes Aircraft Company. And when his *will* to win was finally matched with a *way* to win—WIN he did! He won time and time again, following *The Right Brain Way*.

Knowing what he knew about the accuracy of Right Brain Research and acting on the recommendations was neither difficult nor risky. For Tom Wittenschlaeger, taking this action was simply the next logical step in winning the business!

Whether you are a CEO, CMO, VP or Director, a brand manager, an account executive or research manager, and you have the will to win, there is a logical, straightforward and scientifically proven *way* to get the job done, no matter how difficult your challenges appear to be! If more C-level and brand executives were able to trust and act on the results of their research and strategy in the way Tom Wittenschlaeger did, three things would happen:

1. Their brands would grow more quickly, with increased profit margins.

2. They would experience greater professional growth.

3. They would enjoy their jobs a whole lot more.

Bill Bernbach knew it almost thirty years ago. Don Schultz knows it today. The key to capturing a healthy chunk of the marketplace in any category is to delve into the minds of consumers and understand at an emotional level what motivates them to buy. You have to answer the "why" questions. Developing this insight into the emotional makeup of consumers is a fundamental part of long-term business success.

Your brand presents you with a gift—the gift of the opportunity to reach out to consumers and communicate at an emotional level. The heart of a brand is wrapped up in how it makes people feel while thinking about it, dreaming about it, looking at it and shopping for it. The way it makes people feel is driven by emotional needs. Great brands allow people to fulfill deep-seated emotional needs.

Understanding that consumer behavior is driven by emotional needs is the first step to following The Right Brain Way and supercharging your business. The next step is to uncover the overriding emotional drivers in your category. In other words, consumers in your category are looking to fulfill several overriding emotional needs as they make their decisions. How do you know what these needs are? You cannot assume you know. You cannot guess. You have to listen with an open mind to your customers in order to discover the answer. And, as you listen, you cannot take what they say at face value.

Once the emotional motivation is identified for a category, you can develop a complete understanding of your brand's position in the minds of consumers. Your brand's position must be a claim to unique territory in the consumer's mind, providing immediate recognition of the brand and instantly communicating the benefits of the brand. The best positions have a strong right brain component, establishing a link between the brand and an emotional need.

Always keep in mind that brand is not literal; it defines the relationship between you and consumers. And like all relationships, there are expectations. There is always an implicit promise driving consumer expectations. You must show how your brand will meet those expectations and the consumers' emotional needs.

Once you have uncovered the emotional needs, identified the brand's position and articulated the implicit brand promise, you can develop a blueprint to guide all creative execution that expresses the brand.

Discovering consumers' emotional needs cannot be left to trial and error, assumptions or superficial methods. The Right Brain Way is an objective, in-depth, substantive and proven method based on how the mind works. The left side of the human brain houses logic and language. The right side of the brain is the seat of emotion and motivation. The left brain responds to words. The right brain responds to pictures. Because the educational system in our country focuses on left brain skills, most business leaders and decision makers are more comfortable with logical, statistical ways of analyzing and addressing business challenges. This focus is half right, but it misses the other half of the picture. Without the entire picture, you are missing half of the tools that you need to build a successful brand. Understanding how the right brain and the left brain work and how they interact provides the foundation for business success today.

APPENDIX A

Planning a Research Project

One aspect of the paradigm for marketing research in business is an implicit set of rules for how to plan, design and conduct a market research project. The rules include a set of questions that have become traditional for the planning of quantitative research projects beginning with the following:

- How many respondents do you need for a high level of confidence?
- Is the sample projectable?
- How do you structure a national probability sample?
- What ethnic groups do you include and how many of each—African-Americans, Hispanics, Asians, etc.?
- What about other demographic variables such as age, education, income, etc.?

Frequently, people forget that these are criteria for quantitative research and they try to apply them to qualitative projects, which is not only unnecessary, but also confusing. It often leads to the attempt to squeeze numbers out of qualitative research, which can only lead to invalid conclusions. In order to understand when these five questions are appropriate and when they are not, we will look at a real-life research project.

Recently, a marketer at a pharmaceutical client asked his research department to find out why the physicians were not writing more scripts for his brand. Here are the objectives that our client, the researcher, gave us. The marketing team for the brand in question developed them:

1. Understand why this group of specialists become doctors
2. Uncover the emotional needs these specialists are satisfying by their choice of profession
3. Understand the emotional drivers influencing their script writing
4. Explore how doctors feel about their decisions and identify their anxieties
5. Identify the most powerful emotional needs driving their behavior
6. Discover the segments within the specialty
7. Determine the size of each segment
8. Define the script writing behavior and decisions by segment
9. Measure the perceptions of the company's brand and chief competitors by segment
10. Identify brand preferences by segment

There are ten objectives here – the first five are appropriate for qualitative research, while the second five are appropriate for quantitative research methods. Mixing or confusing the two by trying to assign numerical values when conducting qualitative research or trying to infer motivations from quantitative methods, without conducting in-depth qualitative first, are two of the sources of invalidity in market research today.

It may seem that this is obvious and that it could not happen very often, yet it is surprising how many times we hear about marketers asking to collect quantitative data in focus groups. And, it is even more common for marketers to think that they know what is motivating their customers by analyzing the findings from quantitative research, specifically, by looking at the patterns of product related attributes in these surveys.

The reason that marketers sometimes confuse the objectives of qualitative research with the objectives of quantitative research is that they rely automatically on the rules of the paradigm that we mentioned earlier. So, they sometimes ask traditional questions appropriate for a quantitative project when conducting a qualitative project, even though the questions are only appropriate for quantitative research.

Let us look first at how to address the qualitative portion of this pharmaceutical project. First, we need some basic information about the physicians in the target market in order to define the recruitment parameters:

- The number of scripts physicians write on all brands in the category each month
- The number of scripts the physicians write for the client's brand each month
- The minimum number of scripts in the category and for the brand per month in order to qualify for the project
- The criteria for defining the target market for the brand
- The types of patients the physicians must see in order to qualify for the project

The approach is to define the types of doctors to be interviewed very narrowly in order to obtain the richest possible information as to why doctors choose the drugs that they do. Contrast this approach to drawing a national probability sample, in which everyone has an equal chance of being included.

Then, using the Right Brain Approach, we look for similarities in emotional needs and barriers among the physicians. We do not compare and contrast physicians across dimensions such as gender, age, type of practice, race and geography, because these are quantitative issues. Instead, we look at the deepest level we can when we look for the similarities among the respondents. Fortunately, when we probe the depths of what goes on inside people emotionally, we find that they are more alike than different. We find that the deeper we go towards understanding motivation, similarities emerge and differences wash out.

Here is a hypothetical example to illustrate the point: when a two year-old girl who is not wearing a life jacket falls out of a rowboat into the water, her mother is terrified. At this level of emotional reactivity, in a situation where a child's physical survival is threatened, all mothers react the same way. Age, race, education, and income, size of house or apartment, marital status, number of other children – none of these things matter at all. The emotional needs and fears that drive all mothers to try to rescue their children in this situation are not only similar, they are identical.

In nearly all product and service categories we find that similarities are pervasive in much the same way. As long as we are probing deeply into the mind and as long as we are focusing on similarities, we do not need large numbers. We do not need a large sample.

Once we have answered our client's first set of objectives with qualitative research, it will be possible to answer the second set of questions posed by the marketing team with quantitative research.

At this time the five traditional questions used in quantitative research listed on page 147 come into play directly and govern the design and structure of a segmentation project.

The five questions form the backbone of most statistics courses and are presented in great detail in dozens of textbooks. Most researchers are highly skilled at addressing these questions and answering them. And, most research we see is technically proficient in relationship to these questions.

However, segmentation and other types of quantitative research tend to break down when the research team starts developing the questionnaire.

There is a list of basic rules that almost guarantees a successful quantitative segmentation project when followed:

1. Ask the right questions
2. Ask the questions right
3. Ask the right people
4. Analyze in the right way
5. Determine the findings
6. Develop implications for the business and recommendations
7. Communicate the results
8. Implement the recommendations

Most projects focus on steps 3, 4 and 5. Steps 1 and 2 are often carried out in a vacuum without the in-depth qualitative research needed to determine what questions to ask and how to ask them.

Right Brain Research fills this vacuum. The findings are so rich that there is no danger that the questions asked will overemphasize product features to the exclusion of emotional benefits.

When it comes to step 6, the implications and recommendations are often weak. Without measuring emotionally based dimensions and attributes, there is little chance of bringing exciting new strategic direction to the marketing team.

Step 7 has traditionally been strong in marketing departments, but lately people are so rushed and frantic that this step is beginning to suffer.

Step 8 is the Achilles Heel of marketing and market research. When the findings are uninspired and expected, people tend to move on and make decisions just as they had before the research project. Each decision is made based on opinion rather than sound consumer research. Tension develops with the ad agency as the creatives take over the initiative. But, management has little in the way of strategic direction and so cannot marshal effective arguments against what is now becoming a creatively driven process.

In conclusion, qualitative and quantitative research supplement and support one another. Ideally, they work together like hand and glove. Typically, a marketer starts with qualitative research to gain an understanding of what is important enough to people for the marketer to measure. Then the project is designed and the questionnaire is written based on this understanding. The results measure things that are important to people — preferences, predispositions, awareness, attitudes, etc. Results uncover findings that need further explanation, which in turn leads to further qualitative research. Both approaches are needed and both approaches produce valuable results.

APPENDIX B

Why Small Samples Work So Well!

Some Right Brain Research projects have as few as 16 interviews per cell. Some market researchers and marketers may be surprised to discover that reliable results can be obtained from such small samples. The real surprise is that reliability and confidence levels can actually be higher for small samples in qualitative research than for larger samples in quantitative research.

Let us look at the statistical model that is the origin of the rules for confidence levels and reliability in market research. The model shows that when qualitative research is conducted properly, marketers can calculate the confidence level for their results just as they do for a quantitative project. In fact, it is possible to exceed the levels of confidence typically achieved with quantitative results — and to do so rather inexpensively.

The Statistical Model for Confidence Levels Explains It All

While large numbers of respondents are necessary to poll and predict behavior such as voting in elections, quantification with smaller numbers of respondents serves a different purpose. Analysis of small groups is often used in psychology to learn more about a process that is COMMON TO EVERYONE. Child psychologists, for example, could study how a few children learn to read or to play the piano in order to understand the process, not to predict how many other children will also learn or when they will learn. Similarly, the results of Right Brain Analysis will **not** say how many people will prefer Brand A over Brand B. It will tell us which things will motivate consumers.

And because people are similar emotionally, we can predict that the results will generalize to other consumers.

To illustrate the benefits of in-depth research with fewer respondents, we can carry the analogy of studying how children learn to play the piano a little further. We know that there are qualitative differences in how children learn piano. Some children learn the piano by ear and some learn in a mechanical way. If we have children representing the different styles, our results may be generalized to all children. This is because whenever we deal with qualitative differences such as learning styles, emotional segments, etc., there are only a small number of groups that people fall into. Large numbers of respondents are not necessary, because people within each group are similar on the dimensions we want to analyze, but not necessarily on other dimensions. By gathering a wealth of data about each individual, we learn about the process and the emotional needs and barriers that apply to everyone.

When studying just a few children learning to play the piano, it is possible to develop insights about how children learn, what stages they move through, what the difficult points and hurdles are and how children overcome them.

Similarly, the Right Brain Methodology points to problem areas, areas of confusion and strong emotional reactions consumers have regarding a particular product or service.

On the following page, Table 1 shows the statistical basis for how large a sample is required for a research project. In general, we are studying strong relationships between emotional needs and specific consumer behavior, i.e., those that occur among most of the respondents. Table 1 shows that as the strength of the relationship between two variables increases (the population r), the size of the sample that is required decreases. In other words, the higher the percentage of respondents who evince a specific emotional need or emotional barrier, the fewer respondents are needed for a given confidence level.

Most quantitative projects allow for weak correlations between pairs of variables because there are so many variables to consider. For example, typically gender, age, marital status, educational level, income level, family structure and a host of other variables will be included. Some will be highly correlated or related to one another, some will not be correlated, some will be related to one another to a moderate degree and others will have low but statistically significant correlations. For this reason, required sample sizes are driven up. Look at the lower left-hand quadrant of Table 1. See how large the N becomes, especially when the 95% level of confidence is required for business decisions. For example, a researcher needs 332 respondents to reach the magic 95% level of confidence when the correlations between two of the variables of interest is .20.

When designing qualitative projects, we can build the design and the analysis plan so that small samples will yield reliable results. As described above we define discrete segments of people. And we focus on the similarities among all of the respondents in each segment.

If we decide to analyze the results so that we will only report emotional needs that we find in 8 out of 10 of the respondents (meaning that the correlation on the left hand column of the table is .80), then we only need 13 respondents in our sample to achieve the 95% level of confidence (see the left hand column in the table on the following page).

TABLE 1
Sample Size Needed to Detect r by t Test
At a Significance Level of .05
(Two Tailed)
Desired Levels of Confidence
POPULATION r

	.10	.20	.30	.40	.50	.60	.70	.80	.90
.25	166	42	20	12	8	6	5	4	3
.50	384	95	62	26	15	10	7	6	4
.60	489	121	53	29	18	12	9	6	5
.67	570	141	62	34	21	14	10	7	5
.70	616	152	66	37	23	15	10	7	5
.75	692	171	74	41	25	17	11	8	6
.80	783	193	84	46	28	18	12	9	6
.85	895	221	96	52	32	21	14	10	6
.90	1046	258	112	61	37	24	16	11	7
.95	1308	332	139	75	46	30	19	13	8
.99	1828	449	194	104	63	40	27	18	11

From Cohen, J. and Cohen, P.
Applied Multiple Regression/Correlation Analysis for the Behavioral Sciences, 1975
Level of confidence (called "power" in statistical theory), refers to the probability of rejecting the null hypothesis, or the probability of finding a "true" result. A level of .80, for example, means you can be confident of finding a result 80% of the time.
r = Estimated size of effect in the population

In most Right Brain projects we focus only on those findings (Psychological Dynamics) that appear in at least 80% of the respondents. In a project with a single segment our smallest sample size is 16, meaning that our confidence level is well above 95% in these projects. In cases where we interview more respondents per segment our confidence levels rise to well above 99%.

Based on the statistical model we arrive at the surprising conclusion that small numbers yield very stable and reliable results, and we can have very high levels of confidence in the results. Now this is a surprise, is it not?

The reason that we can work with such small samples with confidence is that we focus on similarities rather than differences among respondents.

APPENDIX C

How Right Brain Research Addresses the Challenges of Qualitative Research

When choosing a method for qualitative research, keep in mind that qualitative research is just as complex and challenging in its own way as quantitative research. It is important to understand the challenges posed by a qualitative project before deciding on which methodology is most appropriate. Some methodologies address these challenges more effectively than others. Right Brain Research is unique in that it addresses all of the challenges effectively.

Challenges of Qualitative Research	How Right Brain Research Addresses the Challenges
Consumers posture, try to appear to be smart and rational about their decisions.	Our analysts bypass the rational or left side of the brain and access the emotional side via visualization techniques.
Consumers want to tell "their stories."	Our analysts guide respondents to focus them on the emotional information we require.
Consumers give rationalizations to justify what they do rather than the real reasons for their decisions and their behavior.	Our analysts probe again and again in different ways to pierce through respondents' rationalizations.

Challenges of Qualitative Research	How Right Brain Research Addresses the Challenges
Often the richest emotional content is contained within seemingly unimportant, casual phrases.	Our analysts are trained to identify emotional language and to probe on it during the interviews.
Brand information is hidden within the category information.	Our analysts are armed with techniques and probes that are proven to yield critical differences in feelings about brands.
Key words identified during interviews always have nuances and implied meanings that are deeper than the literal meanings of the words.	Our analysts are trained to avoid the trap of taking what people say literally, so that they can probe for the deeper meaning that underlies what people say.
There is so much information in an interview and in a body of interviews that it can be an overwhelming task to sort through the material and categorize it.	Our analysts have a framework for understanding and interpreting the material that they uncover in their interviews. This framework is based on identifying the emotional needs and barriers that motivate the respondents' behavior.
Interviewers are naturally tempted to inject their own ideas, feelings and personal experiences into their perceptions and understanding of what they hear.	Our analysts are trained to set aside their personal, subjective feelings about a category or brand and never to make assumptions that could shape their understanding of what respondents mean.
Interviewers naturally want to use their personalities in order to build rapport with respondents—which leads to subjectivity bias and a poorly controlled interview.	Our analysts are trained to relax respondents and gain their confidence by following a carefully structured methodology throughout the interview. Doing so ensures objectivity and consistent findings across analysts.

Challenges of Qualitative Research	How Right Brain Research Addresses the Challenges
Use of one interviewer has the advantage of eliminating differences across interviewers but maximizes the chances for subjectivity bias.	We use three or more analysts who follow a structured and proven methodology, and are supervised by a Senior Project Director, which guarantees that personal bias and subjectivity is controlled and that all of the interviews will be conducted in the same way.

Printed in the United States
By Bookmasters